# RUSKIN

# GREAT LIVES

A complete list of the GREAT LIVES with the authors' names
can be had on application.

DUCKWORTH, 3 Henrietta Street, London, W.C.2.

# RUSKIN

*by* GERALD CROW

Great Lives

DUCKWORTH
3 HENRIETTA STREET
LONDON          W.C.2

*First Published . . 1936*
*All Rights Reserved*

Made *and* printed *in* Great Britain
*By* The Camelot Press Ltd
London *and* Southampton

# CONTENTS

5

# CHRONOLOGY

1857.   *The Elements of Drawing.*
        *The Political Economy of Art.*
        Work on Turner's drawings at National Gallery.
1858.   First meeting with Rose La Touche.
        Un-conversion at Turin.
        Hon. Student of Christ Church.
1859.   *The Two Paths.*
1860.   *Modern Painters*, Vol. V.
1862.   *Unto This Last.*
        *Munera Pulveris.*
        Death of Elizabeth Siddal.
1864.   Death of John James Ruskin.
        *Sesame and Lilies* (published 1865).
1866.   Proposal of marriage to Rose La Touche.
1867.   *Time and Tide.*
1868.   *The Mystery of Life and its Arts* (Dublin lecture).
1869.   First Slade Professorship.
1871.   St. George's Fund.
        *Fors Clavigera.*
        Hon. Fellow of Corpus.
        Purchase of Brantwood.
        Elected Lord Rector of St. Andrews.
        Death of Margaret Ruskin.
1873.   Re-elected Slade Professor.
1874.   Road-making at Hinksey.
        Tea-shop at Paddington.
        Studies Giotto at Assisi.
1875.   Death of Rose La Touche.
1876.   Re-elected Slade Professor.
        Studies Carpaccio at Venice (St. Ursula).
1878.   Brain-fever (Feb.).
        Whistler *v.* Ruskin.
        Resigns Slade Professorship.
1880.   Nominated for Lord Rectorship of Glasgow.
1881.   Brain-fever (Feb.).
1882.   Brain-fever (Mar.).
1883.   Re-elected Slade Professor.
1884.   *The Storm Cloud of the Nineteenth Century.*
1885.   Resigns Slade Professorship.
        Brain-fever (July).
1886.   Brain-fever (July).
1888.   Brain-fever (Dec.).
1889.   Brain-fever (Aug.).
1900.   Death at Brantwood (Jan. 20).

TO
WILFRED CHILDE

# CHAPTER I

A literary way with experience – an age propitious to the tractable – origins conducive to matriarchy – mamma manufactures a clergyman – papa fosters a poet – cousins, safe and unsafe – verse and vignette behind horses, at home and abroad – a literary wooing – a Romantic manufactures himself.

" MY DEAR PAPA.

" A good Newyear to you. I at first intended to make for your Newyears present a small model of any easily done thing and I thought I would try to make an orrery but at length I gave it up on considering how many different things were wanted and composed the inclosed poem with another short address to you but Mamma disliking my address and telling me to write a small letter to you I attempted though I will not say I have succeeded to do it which thing I hope you will accept however unworthy it be of your notice

" dear papa
" your affectionate son
" JOHN RUSKIN

" Hernhill
" *December thirty first 1828.*"

Nothing could better illustrate the tenor of Ruskin's early training than this letter, beautifully

penned by a child nearing his tenth birthday.[1]
It is disconcerting.  For a child to inhabit two
simultaneous worlds, those of his own imagination and of customary intercourse, is nothing
unusual.  But here is most evidently made the
powerful, if unrealised, discovery that the gulf
between these worlds can be bridged from the
*further* shore, from the sovereign state of the mind,
by the instrument of deliberate literary composition.  It is with a real dignity, therefore, that he
recounts two humiliations of the actual world –
that he cannot make an orrery and that he must
submit to mamma.  Each time, he relegates his
embarrassment to a subordinate construction ;
but in so doing he does evade the sense of limitation, as if it belonged to an inferior world.  And
yet so openly does he live that, instead of indulg-
ing secret consolations, he can embody the
matter in a New Year letter to papa, under the
eye of mamma, and reimport the whole trans-
action into the actual world.

This is a clue to so much of Ruskin's strength
and weakness that it is worth while firstly to trace
its discoverable beginnings and, afterward, to
follow where it leads.  How came he to be composing letters, and such letters, to a father under
the same roof ;  how to talk with such familiarity
of making orreries ;  how, again, to mark the
occasion with an ode and an address ?  And how

[1] This letter is published in facsimile in *The Poems of John
Ruskin*, ed. W. G. Collingwood (George Allen, 1891), Vol. I,
facing p. 20.

did this knack of manipulating experience avail him finally in the larger world? In his later years, Ruskin himself returned to the recollection of his origins and wrote of it, with this same sedate detachment and with an unhurrying charm, in *Præterita*, where no one should lose the pleasure of seeking it.

In point of time, Ruskin came very near to being Queen Victoria's exact contemporary. He was born fifteen weeks earlier than she, on February 8, 1819, while his death on January 20, 1900, preceded hers by a year and two days. He was born, therefore, to a great Liberal epoch, an age of ideas; one, moreover, of external security, since Waterloo, but of interior apprehensiveness, thanks to the French Revolution, wherein ideas had shown themselves peculiarly explosive. Hence, while it was a time particularly favourable to the emergence of men of ideas, we should expect to find it, in the main tendency of those ideas, increasingly law-abiding and, in consequence, affording a maximum protection to the life and property of individuals, upon condition of their feeling a like tenderness for these objects of solicitude. And under such protection the less self-reliant types encountered their fullest opportunity. Now tendencies of this kind had their characteristic bearing on the education of children; for an especial tightness of parental authority accompanied a corresponding freedom of individual parents to bend the twig in conformity with their singular preference. Catholic Church and corporate State both claim to preside over this relation and to subject both parent and child to their own discipline for their own ends. But at this time, when the abrupt industrial demarcation of the social classes was beginning to be felt, the only rigid body of doctrine to which the parental caprice could be referred was family tradition or the practice of a particular class. The gradations of religious belief were, by now, infinite.

These facts bore rather obliquely upon Ruskin, because his family tradition was disastrous, and his mother, who took almost entire control of him, was somewhat ill at ease on her husband's social and cultural level. Briefly, Ruskin was the son of first cousins. His paternal grandfather and his maternal grandmother were brother and sister. The brother made a romantic marriage with Catharine Tweddale, a lady of good family, and mixing with admirable burgess society in Edinburgh so mismanaged his wine-merchant's business as finally to commit suicide, leaving a mountain of debts. The sister, on the other hand, addressing a shrewder talent to more modest ends, figures as Mrs. Cox, keeping with pronounced success the old King's Head Inn at Croydon. By the untimely death of Captain Cox, a sailor much absent from home, she was left to provide for two young daughters, of whom Margaret, the elder, was not yet nine. At the age of twenty, Margaret was summoned to keep house for her unbusiness-like uncle in Edinburgh, her cousin John James Ruskin being then sixteen. These two were married some seventeen years later and became Ruskin's parents. Margaret had attended a genteel local day-school and became the model of its narrow, though not contemptible, perfections. Her cousin was put to the famous High School in the Scottish capital and won the sympathetic interest of Dr. Thomas Brown, Professor of Moral Philosophy at the University. While, therefore, Margaret's family tradition was one of successful feminine dominance and strict Evangelical principles, her husband's was one of romantic paternal mismanagement, in which the Evangelical principles, though present, were tempered by wide culture and the graces of a by no means Philistine society.

Promoted to an unfamiliar level, Margaret with her inelastic training evinced a little shyness in her new world, a little stiffness with the old. In consequence, as will be seen, the intimacies of her home were jealously guarded, and Ruskin's boyhood was unusually solitary. To the end, Margaret watched every new influence upon her son with invincible suspicion. Another reason for this exclusiveness conduced, also, to her un-challenged ascendancy : her husband, in paying off his father's debts and building up his own London business of Ruskin, Telford & Domecq, had very seriously impaired his health.

Margaret was thus free to mould John Ruskin precisely as she chose : her own tradition was manifestly less perilous than her husband's, and she had far more energy available for its enforcement ; there was no religious check on her, a consciously religious and exemplary woman who had allowed herself all too little occasion to feel a sense of sin ; there was little social check, for she had erected her own barriers against society. Hence it is necessary to examine Margaret's mind and method more closely.

Her uncompromising rigidity betrays the fact that she had put her eggs into the wrong basket and was uneasily aware of it. Ruskin himself points an incisive contrast between Margaret and her sister :

" My mother was then seven or eight years old, and, with her sister, was sent to quite a fashionable (for Croydon) day-school, Mrs. Rice's, where my mother was taught evangelical principles, and became the pattern girl and best needlewoman in the school ; and where my aunt absolutely refused evangelical principles, and became the plague and pet of it.

" My mother, being a girl of great power, with not a little pride, grew more and more exemplary in her entirely conscientious career, much laughed at, though much beloved, by her sister ; who had more wit, less pride, and no conscience."

Whatever instinct originally apprenticed Margaret to conscientiousness, her sister's good-natured banter made it a matter of conscious principle and unremitting purpose. It destroyed any flexibility of adaptation to the discovery that charm and vitality are better passports to the general affection than is any firmness of principle. To change in the face of ridicule is to lower one's flag and court further laughter. Margaret stuck to her principles. She had all a woman's instinct to maintain herself in the right ; no consequences could seem so fatal as the admission that her whole life was mistaken, that her instincts were not to be trusted. She was at this solid advantage, that her conviction of rightness was backed by substantial virtues and attainments. She had sufficient force of character to impress any society which rose superior to schoolgirl ribaldry. She was not ridiculous ; she was formidable. Above all, she was eminently " sensible," in no way romantic, emotional, or passionate. It was a life completely dominated by the mind ; in many directions, unfortunately, by the mind of a schoolgirl. During the nine years of her engagement she " showed her affection chiefly in steady endeavour to cultivate her powers of mind, and form her manners, so as to fit herself to be the undespised companion of a man whom she considered much her superior." She knew her own limitations.

Her relation to her husband is interesting. When he was " a dark-eyed, brilliantly active,

BR

and sensitive youth of sixteen, she became to him
an absolutely respected and admired – mildly
liked – governess and confidante. Her sympathy
was necessary to him in all his flashingly transient
amours ; her advice in all domestic business or
sorrow, and her encouragement in all his plans
of life.'' It is evident that she had the good sense
not to avenge her sister's ridicule upon him. And
he in his turn thought her, when the time came,
though not an ideal heroine, quite the best person
to have as a wife : an arrangement which pleased
her very well. While he must have felt himself
valuably steadied and directed by her influence,
his own abilities were considerable. A long letter
of advice from Dr. Thomas Brown excludes all
doubt of that. Unfortunately his energies were,
perforce, loyally concentrated upon his business,
to some neglect of a cultural life he was well
adapted to pursue.

We can descry the road Ruskin was ordained to
travel. Both parents had ambitions for the son
who was available to fulfil their two, mercifully
not incompatible, day-dreams. The father
wanted to realise in his son the disappointed side
of his own nature. The mother destined him to
vindicate, in the world of masculine endeavour,
the principles of her own undeviating life. Each
wanted to inhabit and animate his existence ;
which, in such harmony as ruled between them,
they could essay with little fear of conflict. But such
dual occupation entailed a deftness in barricading

the child's latent self into an appointed alcove. And so, in actual fact, events physically proved.

Margaret devoted her son to God, before he was even born. " Very good women are remarkably apt to make away with their children prematurely, in this manner." She meant him for an Evangelical clergyman. Her treatment of him was curiously impersonal ; so much so, indeed, that she became like a force of nature to him. Her own course was too steady for her to feel the disastrous necessity which impels a mother to provoke in her son such emotional states as adjust the balance of her own. Yet, by reason of its systematic nature, her guidance precluded even a chance evasion of that especial disaster which her sex and outlook least equipped her to foresee. She laid up for her son the eventual shame of finding himself, by her making, something less than a man. From her point of view it was not necessary that he should battle for his own way in life ; he could rise by force of gravity. His financial position was assured. Learning, piety and a dignified bearing would advance him sufficiently in a profession where self-seeking was surely inappropriate, though her theology was not unsympathetic to holding temporal favours the logical recompense of spiritual graces. Accordingly she taught him unhesitating obedience and confined him to the most sedate occupations, forbidding him to run the ordinary risks of healthy boyhood. She conducted him, in daily readings, through the entire Bible, from Genesis to Revelation, again and again, omitting nothing, however disputable its edification. She herself taught him his early lessons morning by morning, and, when they were thoroughly mastered, left him to amuse himself, whipping him if he were fretful or troublesome, if he should cry or fall downstairs. She allowed him almost no toys, and the counting out to him of three raisins was a memorable event. She never told him anything untrue, never withheld anything she promised, never threatened anything that she did not perform. The effect of all this was to throw him entirely upon the resources of his own observations and meditations for entertainment, and at the same time to render him acquiescent rather than critical. He became fascinated by the patterns and shapes of things, by plants in the garden, by the proceedings of bricklayers, stone-sawyers or paviours, or of men filling water-carts. We can trace to this time the hankering after practicality which beset his adult life. And thus early he acquired two faculties which he considered the basis of his analytical power : patience in looking and precision in feeling. What calls for explanation is that, being much restricted and considerably whipped, he found his principal feelings were precise, and were those conjoined to the pleasures of observation. He was neither resentful nor rebellious, nor conscious of being treated more strictly than other children, however natural and healthy such feelings would have been. He lived, it would seem, so powerfully and freely in his own mental world that he could very easily recompense himself there for the limitations of physical life, especially as – and this is crucial – that mental life was recognised and encouraged by his parents, so as to form the most positive and important part of his relation with them, and one in which effort and industry, though not cleverness, were rewarded. He was never afraid that his efforts, however absurd, would meet with banter. At the age of six he began a continuation of Miss Edgeworth's *Harry and Lucy*, with material drawn from Joyce's *Scientific Dialogues* and from *Manfred*. In it " Harry ran for an electrical apparatus which his father had given him and the cloud electrified his apparatus positively after that another cloud came which electrified his apparatus negatively." In a child of six this is formidable. Yet anyone reasonably conversant with the children's books of the period will recognise this as the kind of mental world to which even very young children were then introduced. It is understandable that, in his mind, he should only be deterred from constructing an orrery " on considering how many different things were wanted."

Mercifully, towards evening, humaner influences arrived, in the person of his father. In the mornings, John James would take coach for Billiter Street, whereupon Margaret's household orders would be swiftly given, the Bible-reading and brief lessons attentively surmounted, and the rest of the day was the boy's own, to read, write, build with his bricks of lignum vitæ, or assemble and dismount his two-arched Waterloo Bridge, or, again, to observe and meditate in the garden. At half past four the father returned to dine, and at six the son would join his parents at tea in the drawing-room, barricaded into a recess by the fireplace – " like an idol in a niche " – by a good writing-table which carried his plate and cup and books. At these times his father would read to his mother, while he could either listen or read to himself as he chose. " Thus," he says, " I heard all the Shakespeare comedies and historical plays again and again – all Scott, and all *Don Quixote* ; at which I could then laugh to ecstasy ; now, it is one of the saddest and, in some things, the most offensive of books to me." Other authors were Pope, Spenser, Byron, Goldsmith, Addison, Johnson. He could pick up what he could best assimilate. It is worth while emphasising the freedom he enjoyed here. His mental life was allowed to grow in its own way, neither greatly forced nor at all snubbed, but permitted to monopolise him to the exclusion of robuster activities. In the result, his sensitiveness was precise, not excessive, and he was absolutely frank, open, and sincere, with the confidingness of a young animal unschooled to fear. He was deterred from dangerous things, not as perilous, but simply as disobedient.

This routine was varied by holidays spent with

his aunts, Jessie Ruskin, now married to Peter
Richardson, a tanner at Perth, and Bridget Cox,
now also become Mrs. Richardson, a Croydon
baker's wife. The first of these died, already
widowed, when Ruskin was about ten, leaving
her fourteen-year-old daughter, Mary, to be
adopted by his parents. She had, too, a younger
daughter, named after herself, who was John's
especial ally. " ' Never mind, John,' said Jessie
to me, once seeing me in an unchristian state of
provocation on this subject [being frowned upon
for jumping off a box on a Sunday], ' when we're
married, we'll jump off boxes all day long, if we
like ! ' " But it was not to be. This Jessie died
a little before her mother, and the Scottish days
were over. This aunt was even more Evangelical
than his mother, " a very precious and perfect
creature, beautiful in her dark-eyed Highland
way . . . a pure dove-priestess, if ever there was
one, of Highland Dodona." Ruskin was felt to be
safe at Perth. But Croydon cousins engendered
more suspicion. The eldest, John, superintended
a younger brother's education by mounting him
on a bare-backed pony, " with the simple
elementary instruction that he should be thrashed
if he came off," and taught him to swim by pitch-
ing him like a pebble into the middle of the Croydon
Canal. Here, therefore, he might never approach
the edge of the pond, or be in the same field with
a pony, but was restricted to walks with his
mother or nurse. " If they had given me,"

Ruskin writes elsewhere, " a shaggy scrap of a Welsh pony, and left me in charge of a good Welsh guide, and of his wife, if I needed any coddling, they would have made a man of me there and then, and afterwards the comfort of their own hearts." At sixty-five he could afford to realise it.

But more important interludes were his father's business tours. John James insisted upon supervising everything personally, even choosing his clerks for their inferiority to himself. He had fallen in with Mr. Peter Domecq while a clerk in the office of Gordon, Murphy & Co., where the other was studying the wine-trade, preparatory to setting up his own business. The firm was established, under Ruskin's management, with Domecq's vineyards and Telford's capital. Every summer, Telford took charge of the office for two months, while Ruskin set out in his partner's chariot to visit their country customers, reviewing half the country one year, half the next, and making a visit to Perth possible every second summer. His share in these journeys placed the observant and sensitive child on terms not only of familiarity but of an actual communion with every kind of English summer landscape and summer weather, and he was taken to see most of the castles and great houses near their route. Always they reached their stopping-place in time to dine at four o'clock ; and in the evening he would write up what he had seen, often in verse, and work up from memory his sketches rapidly made on the way. His narrative poem, *The Ascent of Skiddaw*, written at the age of eleven under the evident influence of *Young Lochinvar*, compares by no means ill with its prototype, while, in his seventh year, he was illustrating his continuation of *Harry and Lucy* with "copper-plates." Not, however, until the spring of 1831, when he was twelve, did his ambition to depict the scenes of his travels lead to lessons from his cousin Mary's drawing-master, Mr. Runciman, though his first efforts date from a journey to Dover in 1829. Soon after this, Mr. Telford gave him Rogers' *Italy* with the Turner vignettes, and his father bought Prout's *Sketches in Flanders and Germany* upon their publication in 1833. These two acquisitions had far-reaching consequences. The second occasioned his mother's proposal that their summer tour be taken upon the Continent, and thus brought him his first sight of the Alps. From Telford's gift he conceived his first enthusiasm for Turner, whose drawings he copied, studied and imitated with understanding care. His own *Jungfrau*, drawn on this first tour, reveals his skill as already considerable. His journal of this tour, much beholden to Sir Walter Scott, is at times exasperating. It could have been the vehicle of so much that he was never quickened into feeling :

> *Lo, together loosely thrown,*
> *Sculptured head and lettered stone*

*Guardless now the archway keep*
*To rampart huge and frowning keep.*
*The empty moat is gay with flowers,*
*The nightwind whistles through the towers,*
*And, flapping in the silent air,*
*The owl and bat are tenants there.*

Slashed with its glittering fifth line, this is Pre-Raphaelite. But the carriage rolls on to Ehrenbreitstein. Ruskin uses his poetry, as already suggested, to correct his feelings, not to release them, as an equilibrist's pole, not a vaulter's. After all, papa and mamma are in the audience. He retains, therefore, a sedate balance, feeling at Andernach, to the best of his precision, what it observably warrants him to feel.

About this time his cousin, the Charles Richardson who had been pitched into Croydon Canal, was apprenticed to Messrs. Smith & Elder. From their publications thus brought to Herne Hill, Ruskin became acquainted with the work of Stanfield and Harding ; that of Prout he knew from two engravings in the *Forget Me Not* of 1827. Charles introduced him to Thomas Pringle, the editor of Smith & Elder's *Friendship's Offering*, who in turn introduced him to Rogers and accepted him as a contributor. He was beginning to model his poetry, though not his conduct, upon Byron's, and was nearing his first serious love affair.

The Continental tour of 1833 had ended in a visit to the Domecqs in the Champs-Elysées.

Three years later, M. Domecq was minded to tour his English clientele in person and, meanwhile, left his four daughters with the Ruskins at Herne Hill. The eldest, Adèle, had fifteen years to Ruskin's seventeen. That he should have been dazzled, for all Margaret's lack of apprehension, was natural enough. He had cut no great figure at the first encounter, and she had little cause to fear that Adèle would take notice of him now. He, moreover, was not interested in girls, but only cared for flowers and minerals and the wave-beats of the sea. There was nothing romantic or emotional in any of his human contacts hitherto. Margaret had piloted John James through many a courtship, including one of a Catholic, with eminent success ; and she was not afraid now. But she miscalculated. Her son was not John James, and lacked his father's charm and elasticity, having all too much of Margaret in his composition. In itself the affair need not have spelled disaster. But this was the one strain Margaret's system was ill calculated to bear. It was an unhandy wooing. Alone with his divinity, he was less alone than ever, chaperoned by his sedater self. Under the watchful eye of a natural scientist, an historian, a theologian, an author, he laid the best qualities of his mind before her, as confidingly as before his parents. He had forgotten how to jump off boxes. He played his old trick, and from the powerful kingdom of imagination wooed her on paper with

*Bandit Leoni* and *Giuletta* and a story about Naples. For the first surprising time, his compositions were ridiculed. He went a step further and wrote a Shakespearean tragedy, *Marcolini*, depicting himself as stern and aloof, yet one whose heart is like a heaven, who can far more easily be, than find, a friend. This state of unsuccessful love was peculiarly necessary to him now. There was no going back. He had realised the divine commonplace of every romantic lover, that his divinity is truly immanent in all the natural world, so that, if he lose her, " Broken is the summer's splendid heart," veritably as his own. His retreat was cut off. Nothing could any longer have the same objectivity. It was not success in love that he wanted, or even understood ; it was that brilliant landscape lit by the beloved smile, or that other, gazed upon by a man locking sorrow in his breast. This was quite essential to his poetry, as a means of reimporting manipulated experience into the actual world. He could not say with Keats, " I *will* resent my heart having been made a football," and go on writing, because he must needs get what he wrote accepted by the person at whom it was aimed. And Adèle would have none of it. It is a melancholy reflection that, although literature cannot teach the Romantic an acceptable mode of wooing, which is a matter for co-operation, it can teach him to perfection the solitary pastime of renunciation. When the time came, Ruskin renounced nobly a

hope which had never been, in any real sense,
a prospect.

> *Let silence guard, with calm control,*
> *The grief my words were weak to tell*
> *And thine unable to console.*

It guarded it through 340 further lines. There
was still that wretched hankering to make this
nobility real by inducing Adèle to recognise it.
He nursed the memory through four years.
Much was written and much published. When
her marriage bade him tear her image from his
heart, he wrote in *Agonia* :

> *But what shall guide the choice within,*
> *Of guilt or agony –*
> *When to remember is to sin,*
> *And to forget – to die ?*

Impossible to console himself elsewhere. For
when the landscape is irradiated by a succession
of luminaries, it becomes apparent that the
phenomenon has its origin in the heart. He was,
in effect, intolerably trapped. Hitherto, girls had
been as " genuine," direct, and sincere as himself. Adèle's graces and instinctive arts could
only seem to promise a more ethereal kindness.
He had been so continuously encouraged to
accept what he was told, that he could not dis-
cern the utter falsity of romantic literary sentiments, of hopeless faithfulness, of noble sorrow.
He had been allowed to falsify his experience and

incorporate the result in his real relations with other people. His parents had behaved like forces of nature, so that he must equally, to his undoing, rely on others to be what they seemed. Yet the noble sentiments were neither truth nor wholly pretence. He made them true, by relentlessly using poetry to force himself to feel what he supposed he ought. Feelings were becoming *desiderata* to him instead of *data*. Margaret worked in him, where she least hoped, causing him to frap down, with a sense of duty remorseless as her own, feelings which in his father's nature found reasonable play. He was nailing his heart to the mast. His salvation was that he could, and must, continue writing. Poetry was the instrument of this crucifixion. It would be published ; Adèle, papa, mamma would read it ; it would touch innumerable Young Ladies sighing over *Friendship's Offering*. He was making himself, in real fact and for practical purposes, one who can far more easily be, than find, a friend. He was being noble ; he was being a goose ! But, if any salutary marksman had paraded his skill by disabling this swan-flight of goose-pride, the eventual golden eggs might have continued unlaid. He had something disarming in his bearing to protect him, a shy grace and a veritable dignity. He had been whipped out of being fretful and troublesome before he could show much strength of it.

# CHAPTER II

By the time of his going up to Oxford, in January 1837, his parents had done well by Ruskin, not less by chance than by design. Except in learning, they had, by too ready an anticipation, equipped him for the society in which he might rather expect to move at the close of his undergraduate career than its inception. Despite the disfigurement of his lower lip by the scar of a dog-bite,[1] he had good looks of a sensitive and studious kind. He was lifted above monetary cares ; he was frank and open, without being demonstrative. If there was stiffness rather than easiness in a bearing which was, nevertheless, well bred, there was the less likelihood of his abandoning himself to social distractions. His settled habits were of piety without ardour, of compliance without servility, of industry without ostentation. He was accurately observant and well versed in

[1] The consequence of a serving-man's neglect of Mrs. Ruskin's express injunctions.

English and European travel. While his tastes were formed upon approved literary models, there was nothing squeamish in the censorship of his reading. He could express himself in writing with ease and confidence, being already one of Pringle's authors ; and Pringle drove, for his kind of public, a surprisingly good team. Moreover, there was behind him, in the paternal sherry, a more than sound, indeed a notable, wine : he knew the temperate and respectful use of it. There was nothing dashing or masterful in him to portend a success with women beyond a clerical degree of seemliness. He was too faithful to his satisfactorily distant charmer – with whom, by the way, Domecq was quite willing for him to prosper, if he could – to seek further opportunities of being unrequited nearer home. He could be relied upon to nurse his companionable sorrow and still accomplish his appointed task. Altogether, he was well adapted to a cultivated, somewhat formal, masculine society whose members are careful of one another's dignity in the punctilious preservation of their own. And surely Oxford, of all places, must be permeated with urbanity. Was it possible that a don should be a rancorous and sardonic eccentric, or an undergraduate a riotous and dissipated prodigal ? In any case, mamma would see him through.

On the other side of the balance, his health was indifferently robust and, though his mind was

not negligibly furnished, his academic schooling
was deficient : he was fortunate in having worked
steadily and intelligently, but not under pressure.
Apart from the deprivation of all really energetic
pursuits, his childhood was marked by at least
three serious illnesses : a feverish complaint at
Dunkeld in 1827 or the following year ; an
apparently protracted indisposition in 1829 ;
and a dangerous attack of pleurisy in the spring
of 1835. If his mother's solicitude was not fully
justified by these experiences, events were to prove
its continuance at least fortunate. In his education her early labours were supplemented by
some teaching in Greek from Dr. Andrews of
Beresford Chapel, Walworth, whose daughter, he
notes, made him aware of " something in girls
that I did not understand, and that was curiously
agreeable." In 1833 he was sent to school in the
mornings with the Rev. Thomas Dale, in Grove
Lane. His school-fellows were few and he saw
little of them . Twice a week, in the evenings, he
got some crumbs of French and a good grounding
in mathematics from a Mr. Rowbotham – discon-
solate, poverty-stricken, asthmatic, a denizen of
Walworth. So slender were these beginnings that
Ruskin's father was advised by the Christ Church
authorities to enter him as a Gentleman Com-
moner, rather than hazard examination – an
expedient fully consonant with the father's
ambition to have the best, as he conceived it, for
his son.

CR

If it was an optimism especially pardonable in a Scotsman, to postulate respect for learning in the atmosphere of a university, no great harm was done. The Gentlemen Commoners, though mundane, were not hooligans ; and there was little fun to be had from ragging Ruskin. He had too swift an inner mechanism for transforming humiliations. Moreover, he was not censorious, not a reformer, not a prig. True, he was for the Church ; but zeal was not the cut of the Cloth in the late 'thirties. And he had been so trained that impulse to action came, not from within himself, but from the society within which he acted, from the family, the university, and later, it was to be hoped, the Church : from himself proceeded the resolution to act, when so impelled, with full tenacity.

He was, it would seem, somewhat harried, even at that date, for abstinence from athletic pursuits ; and it had to be impressed upon him that, while to stump his tutor with an awkward question might enhance the prestige of his order, to engross fifteen minutes of a Saturday afternoon by having a weekly essay chosen for public reading was in inferior taste. He was so far astray in posing as more easily befriending than befriended that he won much acceptance by his unusual skill in drawing, his enthusiasm for science, and a native imperturbability nothing short of aristocratic. When a riotous party broke down his oak and invaded his bedroom late at night, he received

them with a precise and amicable speech :
" Gentlemen, I am sorry that I cannot entertain
you now as I should wish ; but my father, who
is engaged in the sherry trade, has put it into my
power to invite you all to wine to-morrow evening.
Will you come ? "

It is proper to remark that, though his mother
took the unusual course of presiding over his
undergraduate career from rooms at 90 High
Street, whither his father repaired at week-ends,
he felt little embarrassment, and, so completely
*sui generis* was he privileged to be, was given
occasion for none.

He was made most readily welcome by dis-
cerning elders. Henry Acland befriended him ;
Dr. Buckland, the Reader in Geology, introduced
him to his confreres, including Charles Darwin,
with whom he gave a good account of himself ;
the future Dean Liddell admired his drawings,
and brought the collection of Old Masters in the
College Library to his notice ; the picture-
galleries at Blenheim were open to him ; Charles
Newton sought his services and retained his
friendship.

His normal day comprised chapel, with perhaps
an hour's reading beforehand ; breakfast at nine,
followed by lectures until one ; luncheon and, at
two, some professorial lecture ; a walk until five ;
attendance at his mother's lodging by seven, when
she took tea ; he would return to college when
Tom sounded, and read for about an hour until

ten. Thus a good deal of steady work was accomplished in classics, mathematics, philosophy, geology. He successfully negotiated Smalls in March 1838.

Meanwhile he was nursing his devotion for Adèle, who entered a convent-school near Chelmsford in 1838 and spent occasional holidays at Herne Hill. He continued to write poetry. His first published verses were in *Friendship's Offering* of 1834, his last in Heath's *Book of Beauty* of 1846. In 1839, at his third attempt, he won the Newdigate. Apart from this distinction, he enjoyed a vast esteem as a contributor to a number of the polite annuals which thronged the period. Yet, although remarkable powers must be conceded to him, they were not enough ; he was almost a poet. And it is not difficult to see the reason. Only in the case of scenery and natural objects would he accept experience simply as given ; and there, as he says, he had " precision of feeling." In the more vital experiences of life he fell a victim to the fallacy that his feelings – of all things ! – might do him credit. Instead, therefore, of manipulating experience solely with a view to, and to the point of, its assuming poetic form, he radically changed it into a more creditable *emotional* form, fixed it in a copy of verses, and tried to actualise and live up to it for ever after. In consequence, he never looked to his models for some more vital way of expressing himself, but rather for some alien mode of feeling already conjoined to its appropriate form. It was a way – and, since he had a good deal of facility, a successful way – of controlling his behaviour and keeping his outward life serene, by muffling his sharper urgencies. Had he found his feelings truly yet discreditably bitter, and conceived it his duty, not even to express, much less to publish, them, as pretty a conflict might have arisen as could wholly obsess his mind to the destruction of its major usefulness. He was fortunate ; but it was not poetry. He did achieve really skilful adoptions of every poet's sentiment and manner that attracted him, with occasionally a passage which his original might have owned, if not have envied. Even at the age of eleven he wrote a poem arguing himself into not mourning for his cousin Jessie ; we find him tormenting himself into every conceivable propriety of sentiment over Adèle ; we find gruesome poems upon subjects from Herodotus, which gave him some distorted outlet. His appropriate audience really became the pale, exoptate version of Adèle, capable of being touched to admiration by the delicacy of a regard too little impetuous to engross her heart ; it became, indeed, the ideal reader of the annuals, the Victorian Young Lady. He preserved, by these expedients, the usefulness of his mind for his fellows, but not for himself. His emotional life was mortgaged to that Impossible She, and he was not destined to redeem it.

Where that usefulness lay remains to be considered. His expectation was to sit for his degree
in 1840 and, doubtless, qualify himself for ordination two years later. His work, though regular,
was not all concentrated on his ultimate goal,
while much time had been given to poetry and at
least some to the Union. After winning the
Newdigate he found himself with a year in which
to ensure a brilliant degree. He began to work
with great intensity ; his tutor, Osborne Gordon,
reading with him in vacation. During this year
negotiations were in progress for Adèle's marriage
to Baron Duquesne. By no duplicity could
Ruskin, pending his examination in June, be
hoodwinked as to the nuptials of March 1840,
which did not, he says, crush him as much as he
expected. After all, it was only the confirmation
of his despair. But it disorganised him completely. Correctness adjured him to renounce
even his renunciation, and commit the treason of
allowing the possible existence of even a second-
best to Adèle. It was inadmissible to hanker
after a married woman. Yet, to forget was to
abolish at a stroke his painfully constructed figure
of himself. To remember was to sin ; and to forget – to die ! In any case, the dilemma did
virtually destroy the poet ; and the loss of him
was a consternation to the man. And he was tied
to the wheels of his own curriculum – or so he
thought – for months to come. His health, never
robust, proved unequal to the dual strain ; he

coughed, and there was blood in his mouth.
There would be no brilliant degree now ; no
bishopric either.  But, if his mother's ambitions
were confounded, she was not without consolations.  Already the Tractarians were lamenting
the barren womb and dry breasts of their Spiritual
Mother.  " I beseech you to take nothing for
granted that you hear from these people," Margaret wrote, " but think and search for yourself.
As I have said, I have little fear for you, but I
shall be glad when you get from among them."
In reality, there was no slightest predisposition to
sacerdotalism in Ruskin's mind.  His parents had
never even sought the acquaintance, much less
the personal guidance, of their pastor.  Margaret
believed, and her son with her, that if the whole
Scriptures were deeply implanted in the mind
they would bear their own fruit, under Provi-
dence, through prayer.  Such a persuasion, for
all its piety, offered little indication of precisely
how, beyond certain major avoidances, the whole
personality – mind, heart, and will – can be
maintained in harmony to serve man's ultimate
purpose.  He was already four years gone in an
inordinate affection which he supposed entirely
creditable to himself !  Had he formed any intimate
personal relation with the Tractarians, and been
impressed by their evident saintliness, and had he
given their case, both theological and historical,
some serious attention, he might have convicted
himself of rendering to Adèle the things that were

God's. As it was, he remained suspicious and antagonistic. But neither his rule of life nor his vocation was basically religious. Each was habitual to him.

The present crisis, therefore, stripped him of two essentially false selves, the constant lover and the Evangelical clergyman. He was thrown back upon his parents and upon such artistic and scientific pursuits as accorded with his natural bent. Strenuous work was denied him. In a sense he drifted. He left England in September, with his family, on his first visit to central and southern Italy – to Lucca, Pisa, Florence, Siena, Rome. But he was ill and languid, and the poet was lost ; he no longer saw things with the old eagerness and confidence. He kept his diary, sketched, and wrote up his tour in letters to his friends. But he was not to be tempted by Harrison, Pringle's successor, to give an account of himself in verse. Florence and Rome, where he took fever, failed to arouse him ; and not before he reached Lans-le-bourg, on his way home, did he recover his hold on life.

" I had found my life again – all the best of it. What good of religion, love, admiration or hope had ever been taught me, or felt by my best nature, rekindled at once ; and my line of work, both by my own will and the aid granted to it by fate in the future, determined for me. I went down thankfully to my father and mother, and told them I was sure I would get well."

The Alps had saved him.  At Geneva he began to reproach himself with idleness and to resolve to employ his time profitably.

He reached England in June and, upon signs of returning illness, abandoned a tour in Wales to place himself under the care of Dr. Jephson, of Leamington, who cured him.  He finished *The Broken Chain*, a long poem occupying him since 1839 – " the last poetry I ever wrote, under the impression of having any poetical power."  In the autumn he resumed his reading with Osborne Gordon for his degree.  Too late to sit for Honours, he passed his Finals with such success, in the summer of 1842, that he was awarded an honorary double fourth.

Little though this success advanced him now towards a career, it allowed of his concealing his authorship of *Modern Painters*, in the following year, under the style of " A Graduate of Oxford." By the time the secret was out, his reputation was established and his career determined.  Apart from his poetry, which appeared over his own name or initials, Ruskin was already a prose writer of some reputation in *Loudon's Architectural Magazine*, as " Kata Phusin," author of " The Poetry of Architecture ;  or, the Architecture of the Nations of Europe considered in its Association with Natural Scenery and National Character " (1837–8). In the same magazine he debated the " Convergence of Perpendiculars," and discussed the " Planting of Churchyards," and " Whether Works of Art may, with Propriety, be Combined with the Sublimity of Nature"; this last with reference to the Scott Memorial. But even as early as 1834 he was writing in *Loudon's Magazine of Natural History*, in the year before the first appearance of his poetry. As an artist he received lessons from Copley Fielding and studied more recently under J. D. Harding. Before going abroad after his illness he had been introduced to Turner by Griffith, the dealer, and was, apparently, on terms with Roberts and De Wint. At Rome he had met Joseph Severn and George Richmond. As a water-colourist he had arrived. But he had so arrived while still hoping for ordination. If that was to be forgone, something must take its place. The sherry business manifestly could not do so; for, though methodical, he was not business-like, and he had conceived a low estimate of the commercial mind from his father's business dinners. Moreover, an incident had occurred to diminish his father's confidence in his capacity. John James had gratified his son's zeal for Turner by purchasing the *Gosport* and *Richmond Bridge* for Herne Hill, and by giving him the *Winchelsea* for his rooms in St. Aldate's. Upon his coming-of-age he gave him £200 a year for his personal use. His first exercise of this discretion was, when arm in arm with his father at the old Water Colour Society's private view, to close with Griffith's offer of Turner's *Harlech Castle*, without consulting his father, or even asking the price ; it turned out to be £70, half as much again as his father had given for either drawing at Herne Hill. His father thought this too airy a way of doing business and too inconsiderate a show of independence. But it won an introduction to Turner.

While, therefore, Ruskin was deliberating what course to pursue, another tour was agreed upon, once more to Chamonix. And while Ruskin was questioning whether, with thousands of souls going daily to their condemnation, he could rightly do aught but try to save them, albeit discovering in himself no special fitness for the task ; and while he was still arguing to convince himself that art was ennobling and tended to the glory of God, his hour struck. Before leaving for Chamonix he had seen and admired Turner's Academy pictures for that year, 1842. These canvases were fiercely assailed by the critics, who decried Turner's later manner from its first appearance in 1836. Even then, at the age of seventeen, Ruskin composed an ardent defence which was submitted to Turner and sent by him to the purchaser of one of the maligned works, *Juliet and her Nurse*, instead of to the offending *Blackwood's Magazine*. Ruskin now determined upon a pamphlet to vindicate his idol. It grew into the first volume of *Modern Painters*.

In the task of extracting from this notable work those elements which seem of permanent value, we must be guided, in what we expect from it, by

the circumstances of its composition. Much of
its interest arises from the hastiness of its launch-
ing. Had he been ordained, Ruskin would only
have allowed the claims of his profession to inter-
fere with his devotion to nature and art with a
sharp sense of bereavement. Even now the
reminder of his dedication to God disquieted him.
He had a foot in either camp ; and, before he
could decide where to place his weight, an urgent
championship of Turner forced him into the
open. In this state of indecision, he began to
build a system within which he could procras-
tinate. He asserted simultaneously the priority
of God's claim upon man and the dignity of the
artist in satisfying that claim. Most religious
people would probably allow art to be theologi-
cally indifferent ; harmful to themselves, in
particular cases, if an occasion of sin ; salutary,
where favourable to their spiritual progress. But
they would scarcely erect the idiosyncrasies of
their interior life into canons of æsthetic criticism.
But if art were indifferent, it could not satisfy the
claims of Ruskin's dedication to his Maker. His
system is based upon his Oxford reading, which
gave him some acquaintance with the Scottish
moralists, some with Locke, and a preference for
Plato over Aristotle, understandable in one to
whom Plato's analogies must have made the same
kind of appeal as the Gospel parables. He relies,
therefore, upon a system of " ideas," and adopts
a courageous stand :

" Man's use and function (and let him who will not grant me this follow me no farther, for this I purpose always to assume) is to be the witness of the glory of God, and to advance that glory by his reasonable obedience and resultant happiness. . . .

" I say that the art is greatest, which conveys to the mind of the spectator, by any means whatsoever, the greatest number of the greatest ideas, and I call an idea great in proportion as it is received by a higher faculty of the mind, and as it more fully occupies, and, in occupying, exercises and exalts, the faculty by which it is received."

The combination falls apart, if we grant man some innocent relaxation from the glorification of God, and allow art to be such. It suffers, also, if we hold, as can be mystically urged, that the higher the faculty which is mortified, the greater the merit. Each proposition is tenable separately, but it was vital to Ruskin personally, and to his system, that they should be held jointly – as, indeed, they can be.

Ruskin was by no means a trained philosopher, and appears involved in a certain confusion at this point. He is evidently mindful of Reynolds' position, in his third discourse, regarding Plato's doctrine of ideas. Sir Joshua taught that every species had its " idea," or ideal pattern, to which any given individual was inferior in some particular or other. The *great style*, *genius*, and *taste* are, he says, different appellations of the superior power of grasping this ideal. "They always operate in proportion to our attention in observing the works of Nature, to our skill in selecting, and to our care in digesting, methodizing, and comparing our observations." Now this central Idea, in the strict sense of the term, is claimed, philosophically, to be an ultimate *reality*, eternally more *true* than its individual representatives. But Reynolds inaugurates the confusion by permitting himself the negligence of saying : "The artist is supposed to have ascended the celestial regions to furnish his mind with this perfect *idea of beauty*." He might equally have termed the same pattern this perfect *idea of truth*. But the abstract idea of beauty is by no means equivalent to the abstract idea of truth. This consideration might sufficiently escape the President's audience to admit of their exalting beauty at the expense of truth, in their pursuit of grandeur. It could lead to Keats' impulsive identification, and it opened the door to Ruskin's ostensibly Lockean classification of ideas desirable to be conveyed by a picture, although the picture actually conveys only ideas of colour, extension, etc. The question of what ideas are properly relevant to æsthetic judgments is the starting-point of modern æsthetic criticism.

Yet *Modern Painters* did considerable service in exploring this particular *cul-de-sac*, which led to Ruskin's exaltation of Landseer's *The Old Shepherd's Chief Mourner* as one of the most perfect pictures which modern times have seen. He was betrayed both by his eagerness to refute the charge that Turner's later pictures were untrue to nature and by his personal need for a system. He had to convince himself and his friends that he was serving God, and to controvert established critics, against whom the authority of his name carried no weight. He needed the support of a system and, imperatively, one organised in relation to their chief authority, Reynolds.

Nevertheless, Ruskin's form of definition is of value, if we make the necessary proviso that it is no function of art, as such, either simply to repeat itself or to do what can be done better and more appropriately by something else. We might then say :

" The art is greatest which offers to the mind of the informed spectator, by any means whatsoever, the greatest advance in that kind of experience which art can best and most appropriately offer ; and fresh experience is an advance in proportion as it is received by a higher faculty of the mind, and as it more fully occupies, and, in occupying, exercises, strengthens, and renders more receptive, the faculty by which it is received."

Using the terminology of faculties, without viewing them as necessarily cloisonné, we might rate as man's highest faculty, for exclusively æsthetic purposes, his appreciation of formal aspects. But

Ruskin betrayed his dedication to God, if he ever allowed our purposes to be exclusively æsthetic. Osborne Gordon[1] has much to answer for here ; and Morris was on surer ground in allowing art to quiet men's minds. But Ruskin, obsessed with art's greatness, could not release from its service faculties better exercised elsewhere.

Ruskin's spectator is essentially the informed spectator, and his vindication of Turner actually proceeds somewhat on the lines suggested above. Having proved him the supreme exponent of the more obvious truths about nature, he represents him as offering us experience of a more recondite truth about light as God's creature, which can only be exhibited by the sacrifice of truths already familiar, and only by Turner's methods. We are to trust Turner[2] because of his evident mastery of

[1] See Ruskin's letter to Osborne Gordon in Cook's *Life of Ruskin*, Vol. I, p. 154.

[2] By the kindness of Mrs. W. Scott, of Aldingbourne, I am indebted to Mrs. Brooke-Hunt (formerly Miss Calverley, of Oulton Hall, Yorkshire) for the following facts illustrative of Ruskin's complete faith in Turner :

" Turner was a great friend of Mr. Fawkes, of Farnley Hall, Yorkshire, and frequently stayed there. While there he made a large quantity of water-colour drawings which he gave to his friend Mr. Fawkes. Once, when my father and mother (Mr. and Mrs. Calverley) were staying at Farnley Hall, the great Ruskin was also there. One evening a water-colour of Turner's was produced, depicting cows standing in water. The reflections of the cows were shown upright, instead of reversed. Ruskin was asked if he could explain this. He took the drawing away to another room and pored over it for an hour. Then, coming back, he said, ' I cannot explain it in the least, but if Turner painted it like that, it certainly was as he saw it.'

" Many years afterwards my father was driving over the bridge at the particular spot at which the drawing was taken (he was driving himself in a dog-cart, *en route* from Ilkley Station to Denton Park). As he crossed the bridge over the little

verifiable truths which he thus earns the right to sacrifice. The trend of modern theory is noticeably towards connecting formal aspects in art with the apprehension of reality as a formal integrity. It demands the sacrifice of obvious truths about actuality to this recondite truth about reality. Reality is a mental concept which stands logically behind appearances ; the Creator stands behind them actively. If the implications of regarding actuality as creation were banished, Ruskin conducts quite readily to modern theory.

He accords chief place to Ideas of Relation, which arise from the view that the painter is composing in at least three modes simultaneously – disposing colour on a flat surface, arranging solids in three-dimensional space, and manipulating the world of human thought and feeling. He is thus ready to make painting aspire to the condition of certain kinds of poetry. But, in assuming these ideas to be necessarily conveyed by the picture, he begs the whole question.

shallow river, the Wharfe, he saw cows standing in the water, and their reflections were exactly as Turner painted them, thereby confirming Ruskin's verdict."

Turner's visits to Mr. Walter Fawkes at Farnley Hall were frequent between 1803 and 1820. Mr. Fawkes died in 1825, and Ruskin's visit was paid to his son, Mr. Francis Hawksworth Fawkes in 1851, Euphemia being of the party. The intimacy was broken off at about the time of the annulment of Ruskin's marriage. It was not until 1881 that Mrs. Ayscough Fawkes wrote to Ruskin asking for his portrait, to be placed in the Turner room at Farnley. Ruskin revisited Farnley once only, in December 1884. These facts were communicated to the *Nineteenth Century* (April 1900) by Mrs. Ayscough Fawkes in an article which makes no mention of the drawing to which Mrs. Brooke-Hunt refers.

His first volume, after propounding his general scheme, is mainly devoted to truth in landscape and its release from mere imitation. He was both obliged to this course, because Turner's truth was challenged, and inclined to it, because he was on sure ground. He had studied, analysed, and copied both Turner and nature almost all his life.

His second volume, which appeared three years later, in 1846, was to deal with Beauty, which, he conceived, was drawn from the natural world by the theoretic faculty and idealised, in process of composition, by the imaginative. This idealising is not " beautification," but operates in the interests of imaginative verity. It involves the discarding of lusciousness, and is not altogether irreconcilable with the modern process of abstraction. In a celebrated passage of *Modern Painters* he could adjure the student to go to nature, " in all singleness of heart, rejecting nothing, selecting nothing, scorning nothing." After all, nature was the work of God, and Ruskin had discovered that plants " composed themselves by finer laws than any known to men." But, in the matter of figure-painting, he found his knowledge of the masters deficient ; and, where character and emotion were concerned, he could not consistently exhort the student to go to human nature in all singleness of heart, etc. He set himself to study the great masters of figure-painting and simultaneously to investigate what nobility of character and – for he still believed in it – of feeling really were, and how the great masters expressed it. This time he betook himself to Hooker for his arrangement and, in overhauling his beliefs, was to find himself disconcerted " by the continual discovery, day by day, of error or limitation in the doctrines I had been taught, and follies or inconsistencies in their teachers." In his exhortation regarding nature, he approaches the realisation that subjects cannot be chosen for extraneous qualities, but only for their æsthetic suggestiveness. Yet, while insisting that the highest appeal of art requires thought for its enjoyment, he cannot admit that the requisite kind of thought is concerned with the artist's aims and vision.

Ruskin's criticisms were destined to have especial weight with a new kind of patron, the man of commerce, whose only recourse would otherwise have been to ape the contemporary " grand " taste of the aristocratic collector. Such men, in the full confidence that their success was due to their Christian virtues, could sympathise with Ruskin's appeal to canons other than the purely æsthetic. At the same time, thoughtful men in other walks of life who were chilled by the recommendations of utilitarianism, against which Ruskin tilted, were greatly heartened by this concordat between religion and art. Despite the critics, who were most evidently vanquished in the matter of Turner, the first volume was a triumph. His success brought Ruskin increased confidence and, as was natural, an enhanced receptivity. He was on the watch for material to nourish, and evidence to confirm, his theory. He devoted the three years of preparing his second volume to the study of stained glass and antique sculpture as well as of painting. In 1844 and the following year he made foreign tours which were a revelation to him. The first took him with his parents to Chamonix once again for an investigation of glaciers. And now, on his homeward way, the Louvre discovered to him for the first time the full splendour of the Venetians and Veronese. He writes of the difference between the latter's " fresco-like attainment of vast effect, in spite of details, and Landseer's or any other of our best manipulators' paltry dwelling on them ! " " I have had a change wrought in me," he says, " and a strong one, by this visit to the Louvre, and know not how far it may go, chiefly in my full understanding of Titian, John Bellini, and Perugino, and being able to abandon everything for them ; or rather being *un*able to look at anything else."

The tour of 1845 was of infinitely greater moment. It was the first in independence of his parents' companionship, attended only by a servant and the Swiss guide, Joseph Couttet. His revelation dawned at Lucca and brightened in Pisa and Florence, in a mood very different from that of his first visit. His trend of thought naturally disposed him, for all his Protestant bias, to

sympathise with the spirit of the Primitives. But
he was struck by their sheer mastery, and the
urgency of his championship was redoubled at
seeing these peerless documents peeling and
crumbling away before his eyes, or smashed to
powder by masons. He hurried to make outline
drawings of what he could. " Raphael and
Michael Angelo," he wrote to his father, " were
great fellows, but for all I can see they have been
the ruin of art." The balance was somewhat
restored at Venice by the discovery of the
neglected giant, Tintoretto. He returned to
England, as the champion of the Venetians and
the Primitives, to lead a revolution in English
taste.

More than that, on this tour unshepherded by
his parents, his definite religious faith evaporated.
He could not embrace the creed which had
animated the early Italians, and beside it he
began to feel something starved and narrow in the
more austere Protestant worship. The Primitives
did not inculcate Catholic theology in him ; but
they did fill him with a sense of heavenly glory.
He was lost to Evangelical principles.

At the same time something else awoke in him.
In the recumbent effigy on the tomb of Ilaria at
Lucca he saw the ideal type of the beauty which
had attracted him in Adèle and in the lovely
Miss Tollemache, once seen in the church of
Aracheli at Rome. He turned now from the study
of clouds and stones and of Turner's landscapes

to the consideration of pictures wherein the ideal of womanly beauty played its part. He was in love with Fra Angelico's angels, their faces " without one shadow of earth or mortality about them " ; he was in love with a figure upon a tomb ; and once again something had died in him – this time his faith.

# CHAPTER III

RUSKIN now bestrode the future. He was the progenitor of a system, to attack which was virtually tantamount to a confession of moral obliquity. And it must be remembered that, although Hegel died in 1831, the propagation of his teachings in England still lay with the future. Ruskin's former scruples were of diminished cogency, since, as he pointed out to the somewhat restive Osborne Gordon, he was " slightly heretical as to the possibility of anybody's being damned." His duty to mankind lay in proclaiming the peculiar revelation vouchsafed to him through painting. In an eloquent passage of *Modern Painters* he maintained that Turner was the first and only painter to do justice to the truth about the real radiance of light ; and this when Monet was three years old. At the same time the Italian Primitives were the last painters to do justice to the incomparable radiance of heaven ; almost alone of later painters, the Venetians had not dissipated their inheritance of splendid colour, while some had even sold their birthright for a mess of bitumen. To the man whose heart was like a heaven there was something dreary, calculating, and sordid about pictures with the current moral purpose. He had a nostalgia for radiance.

With the success of his second volume all pretence of keeping the secret of the Graduate of Oxford was at an end. Returning from the Continent in 1846 he found himself famous. Miss Mitford complimented him and received him in the country; Rogers acknowledged him and received him at breakfast; Lady Davy collected him and received him at dinner; John Murray, who had virtually rejected *Modern Painters*, approached him and, in desire but not in fact, received him into the fold. In June he became Secretary to the Geological Section of the British Association at Oxford and, while there, was placed upon Mr. Gladstone's election committee, at his first parliamentary candidature for the university.

But these honours did nothing to advance a cause which now engrossed his heart. Lockhart, whom he met at Lady Davy's, gave him Lord Lindsay's *Christian Art* for review in the *Quarterly*. His wooing of the biographer's daughter, conducted with his usual oblique approach, met with scanty consideration. He aired his views to Gladstone across her at dinner; he laboured to

impress her with his review. The daughter
married J. R. Hope, whose serious rival, except
in imagination, Ruskin had small occasion to
suppose himself ; the father ruthlessly mangled
his review in the *Quarterly*. Once again he was
ill and depressed and his work dragged, though
a month at Leamington with Dr. Jephson restored
him somewhat. Within a year his parents discovered a strange expedient to allay their anxiety
in marrying him to Euphemia Chalmers Gray, the
daughter of a Perth lawyer, a friend of long
standing. Anxious, puzzled, and disappointed
his parents certainly were, and with some reason.
Instead of continuing his work on painting, he
was diverting his attention to Gothic architecture, while, when he might have been augmenting
his reputation as an artist by doing finished drawings as of old, he was making miserable scrappy
notes of architectural detail in hieroglyphs of his
own. What was worse, as his convictions diverged
from theirs, they discovered in him a diminished
confidence towards them. Moreover, nothing
would any longer persuade him into poetry, and
his father, to the son's disgust, collected *The Poems
of J. R.* into the volume of 1850. It was time for
him to be settled. And, even more than to " gain
a daughter without losing a son," they hoped, in
this alliance, by choosing a daughter, to regain a
son. They gave him little less than a sister, and
little more. Miss Gray, herself, evinced an
ominous inclination to capitulate before a

preparation of siege which the guardian of no previous citadel had accounted a sufficient tribute either to the difficulties of the enterprise or to the felicities of its reward. Six years had passed since he had written, at her request, " a fairly good imitation of Grimm and Dickens, mixed with a little true Alpine feeling of my own," his fairy tale, *The King of the Golden River*. The gay, attractive child of twelve had become a beautiful and vivacious girl of eighteen. The invalid of twenty-two, with his degree still to take, was now a famous author, the Graduate of Oxford. But she was in too great a degree his debtor for what, had it derived from other sources, might have made her the partner of his labours : her taste and the cultivation of her mind. Upon her birthday, in May, he wrote :

> *May all earthly sun, sweet sister,*
> *On thy journeying shine, –*
> *Though perhaps there may be, sister,*
> *Shadows upon mine.*

In April of the following year, the Year of Revolutions, they were to put it to the touch, in a less cautious relation than he then claimed, whether he could assist her to, and share in, the sunshine he bespoke. He set about it strangely.

Lord Lindsay's *Christian Art* took cognisance of architecture, and it was proper that the system of *Modern Painters* should be capable of extension to it also. Not only the unity of the arts, but the relevancy of the glory of God to the whole discussion, was at stake. The tour of 1846 took him to Venice, where he sketched and measured ; and in the interval he had expended upon architecture such diligence as disappointment and ill health allowed. The state of Europe in 1848 being such as to imperil, not only the tranquillity of his progress, but the very existence of the buildings and pictures he desired to visit, the return from Scotland after the wedding was interrupted by a visit to the Lakes ; and it was not until August that John James accompanied his son and daughter to Boulogne and saw them off *by rail* on a journey through northern France. There was no triumphal progress across Europe behind horses. It was a changing world.

Any confidence of reclaiming Ruskin from his present ways was indulged only to be disappointed. To spend hours poking about and taking measurements and drawing fragments with loving accuracy was a different thing altogether from making rapid studies and working them up from memory. It made him very bad company for people less engrossed and utterly in the dark about the principles which took excitingly clearer shape in his mind with the discovery of every new corroboration. Ruskin was in love with discovery and with the lovely evidences of the past which the restorer and destroyer were rapidly taking from him. It would have needed a loyalty comparable to Margaret's, a calm and self-sufficiency such as hers, to give Ruskin the kind of wife that his future needed – one who could have ministered to his capacity for working absorbedly and delightedly in his own way. Only had she had a son could such a life have been at all tolerable for her. However popular in Victorian fiction may have been the notion of the husband forming the tastes and character of a docile and pliable wife, Nature has her revenges, ever in Victorian fact. Euphemia's readiness to be guided and impressed by what her predecessors had ridiculed was a biological absurdity. But the prize was by this time a more considerable one. Apart from being the sole child of a really wealthy and not prodigal man, his own position was already established. Conceivably she thought to make something of him after marriage, even if she destroyed all the sources of his happiness over which she did not personally preside and snapped the mainspring of his powers. What he needed was a guiding star ; someone out of his reach, but not beyond his eternal hope. Adèle should have died, to become his Beatrice. Later it was too late.

Ruskin brought his bride home to the paternal roof after three weeks among the Lakes, when he was ready to confess : " I have been committing and causing my wife to commit all kinds of breaches of etiquette, sending no cards to anyone to begin with." With what satisfaction he ! – with what misgiving she ! After correcting the

proofs of the second edition of *Modern Painters*,
and making the inevitable visit to Oxford, he
began a tour of the English cathedrals, apparently
with the additional company of his parents, for
his father writes : " My son occupies himself with
the architecture of the Cathedral [Salisbury], a
lovely edifice, but I find it very slow." Over his
notes and measurements, in an English summer,
he fell ill ; recovering, he sought the more clement
air of Normandy. His only detailed work upon
an English cathedral was that at Salisbury.

The outcome of the tour was *The Seven Lamps of
Architecture*, written, that winter, in his own house,
31 Park Street, Grosvenor Square. Much of the
book, a strangely unequal one, seems the work of
an exasperated captive. Speaking of the end of
his solitary tour of 1845, he wrote in *Præterita*,
long afterwards : " I had scarcely reached home
in safety before I had sunk back into the darkness
and faintness of the Under-World." His biographer[1] interprets the Under-World as " the
falling away in the fervour of his personal faith."
It is possible to dissent from this view, in some
measure ; for, in the same passage, Ruskin says :

" But now, between the Campo Santo and
Santa Maria Novella, I had been brought into
some knowledge of the relations that might truly
exist between God and His creatures ; and
thinking what my father and mother would feel if

[1] E. T. Cook, *The Life of Ruskin*, Vol. I, p. 189.

I did not get home to them through those poplar avenues, I fell gradually into the temper, and more or less tacit offering, of very real prayer."

It was the radiancy of Fra Angelico's heaven which threw him for the first time in his life, ill, voyaging, and alone, into more than perfunctory prayer. He received a " consciousness of answer," and found himself " in the inn at Beauvais entirely well, with a thrill of conscious happiness altogether new to me." " Which," he says, " if I had been able to keep ! . . . Another ' had been ' this, the gravest of all I lost ; the last with which I shall trouble the reader." What followed, we know. The temptation to conclude that it was the loss of this vision, the closing in again of " Evangelical principles," which really weighed him down is sharpened by *The Seven Lamps*, whose first edition contained " some pieces of rabid and utterly false Protestantism " which he excised later. Meanwhile, his experiences had somewhat blurred the schematic outline of *Modern Painters*. His Lamps, though they bear similar names, are by no means the Ideas of the earlier book.

With the scant justice of brevity, his argument is this : If you want a great national architecture – and you ought to want it, since it is your history book and your unmistakable exemplar – you must have a great national consciousness ; that is to say, in wealth or poverty, peace or war, in

barbarism or refinement, under liberal or arbitrary
rule, you must have that community of endeavour
which will produce a school, and you must so
respect each and every citizen as to make his work
at least worthy of, in his highest aspect, the man.
Given this, you must take time into partnership
and build for posterity as your ancestors built for
you, reverently preserving your inheritance and
not falsifying it by restoration, but adding to it
the best and most costly that you can, scorning
deceits in structure, material, and workmanship.
Moreover, you shall know when and how, by
breadth of treatment, thinking in terms of light
and shadow, to win an effect of power ; and when
and how to secure beauty of proportion or
colour ; and when and where beauty of ornament is opportune and appropriate, and how to
achieve it and keep it in its place. Not least, you
shall make all this the living art of men enjoying
their full and true life as men ; an art not en-
slaved to mechanical precision of finish ; but
bold, elastic, a little irregular, capable of using
initiative and of running risks. Go back to the
point where your historic style lost its integrity,
a little before it lost life and beauty, and develop
a style consciously from there, being careful not
to lose it again. When you have done all this,
and then only, you will make your churches an
acceptable gift to your Deity.

But at every turn there is an undercurrent of
exasperated personal protest. If we review the

Lamps in order, that of Sacrifice is a protest against the meanness of the Protestant conventicle, but couched in the only terms the offenders could understand ; demanding sacrifice not gratitude. It is false to his vision. For the mood of Beauvais, had it lasted, would have found happier expression in a Lamp of Thankfulness. He ignores that the Italian painters believed and rejoiced that what was housed in their churches and offered on their altars was substantially their Redeemer, Light of Light, the Living Radiance of his celestial vision, under the figure of bread. He was back in the Under-World. " Truth " rails at the smooth and well-intended hypocrisies of life, and, incidentally, against the meanness of cast-iron ornament ; " Power," at the smallness and meanness of English building. He limits " Beauty " to that of ornament, proportion, and colour ; a useful limitation to which he is fully entitled, provided it be kept clear. And he is inclined to put this kind of beauty in its place : it must not be " thrust into places set apart for toil. Every man knows where and how beauty gives him pleasure, if he would only ask for it when it does so, and not allow it to be forced upon him when he does not want it." Ostensibly this is an argument for what is now called " functional beauty " or " fitness for purpose," that comely, unofficious serviceableness to which Ruskin, with his fondness for moral attributes, might have given, in its undebauched meaning, the name debonair. But this is dangerous talk, underneath, in his first married year. The Greeks had a meaning for Euphemia.[1]

But it is his fifth Lamp, that of Life, which contains his most notable and significant outburst against the false life :

" that life of custom and accident in which many of us pass much of our time in the world ; that life in which we do what we have not proposed, and speak what we do not mean, and assent to what we do not understand ; that life which is overlaid by the weight of things external to it, and is moulded by them ; that which instead of growing and blossoming under any wholesome dew, is crystallised over with it as with hoar frost, and becomes to the true life what an arborescence is to a tree, a candied agglomeration of thoughts and habits foreign to it, brittle, obstinate and icy, which can neither bend nor grow, but must be crushed and broken to bits if it stand in our way."

After being " brought into some knowledge of the relations that might truly exist between God and His creatures," he was being stifled. Again and again he insists that a man's happiness springs from his vision and his work, not, he seems to imply, from his parents, his wife, his friends, his diversions, but his work. The Lamp of Memory rages against the architectural destroyer and restorer ; " Obedience " has its diatribe against

[1] " Abstinence from ill-omened words."

ER

not giving men work that will occupy them men-
tally and satisfy their whole nature, instead of
merely earning for them their pittance or their
crust.

Ruskin was not, despite his eloquence, deliver-
ing a confident message with power ; he was
elaborating a tentative one with incomparable
ingenuity. He was following clues which would
lead him to a goal he would not recognise until
he reached it. And the clues were being obliterated before his eyes. But in this quest he sought
his true self ; and he was exasperated by the alien
views and trivial claims pressed upon him from
without. His passages of eloquence are of the
kind before which it is possible to feel embarrassment. They are not those of mastery, but of
extreme shyness. It was not sufficient for him to
discover and enunciate a dialectical truth. He
must, when he chanced on a substantiation of his
hopes, press it to his heart to see if it would really
fit. For this reason his truths were actually felt ;
and the thought is not wholly extricable from the
feeling. Hence he became, to exhibit his thought
and at the same time master and render decorous
his emotion, elaborately eloquent.

The development of a man's thought is the
history of what is indeterminate acting upon what
is already determined. Ruskin's theory at this
point was fluid within certain rigid boundaries.
He is convinced that the Bible is a whole which
contains the ultimate Truth, and that the Catholic

Church is an institution which does not. He
regards the Apostolic See with an ignorant dis-
respect, whose expression, as he afterwards
realised, disfigures his work at this time. It is not
a native sturdiness ; it is rancour by rote. At
the same time, he is convinced of the primacy of
high principles, as the source of national greatness of character, by which he sets infinite store.
But his widening outlook has engendered grave
doubts about the Evangelical principles imbibed
in his youth. And the diversion of his interest
from painting to architecture has inevitably
raised the question involved in the operation of
building upon a large scale, that of the relation
between master and man, between designer and
executant. The painter is his own executant ;
the architect, like the composer and the drama-
tist, is not. Ruskin's attention is now more concentrated upon this world than the next. It is
not that souls are in danger of hell, but that men
are denied the " true life," a fact illustrated by
his own private experience, which disturbs him.
And from these sources sprang that momentous
book *The Stones of Venice.*

Ruskin was no stranger to Venice, and he felt
for its architecture an admiration which was as
eccentric then as it is customary now. But he was
drawn to it especially, because he believed it to
be the product of a national greatness, in his own
acceptation of the term, specifically anti-papal.
He began, therefore, to brood over the history of

the Venetian State and of its architecture, and he found all in such confusion that he had no choice but to examine every building in detail and wrest his evidence from the stones themselves. After the publication of *The Seven Lamps*, Ruskin went to Chamonix with his parents, with a view to the continuation of *Modern Painters*, while his wife, unequal to the rigours of a Swiss tour, remained with her parents in Scotland. His studies for the third and fourth volumes of the earlier book were made on this tour of 1849. He returned to England in the autumn and conducted his wife thence to Venice for the winter. He returned again to write and publish his first volume of *The Stones*, and was back in Venice for the next winter but one, gathering materials for the two succeeding volumes which completed the work. The book had two manifest consequences : one salutary, the other disastrous. It laid the foundation of the just appreciation in England of Byzantine architecture, and rescued St. Mark's from the contempt and even the ridicule of the polite world. As against this, his ardent researches, his elaborate analyses, his careful measurements, his faithful drawings, all gave the English builder *gratis* a reach-me-down architectural style, whose mechanical exploitation invoked his own irrefragable authority, while extinguishing with seven bushels the spirit of all the Lamps he named. His avowed object had been to show that the decline of Venice dated from the decay, not of her public and ceremonial, but of her private and individual religion. He warned the last of the three great empires of the sea – Tyre, Venice, and England – to heed the fate of the second before her material documents followed her greatness into the desolation which engulfed the first. He was heard and even hailed, but not effectually heeded. The second volume, however, with its famous sixth chapter, established, once and for all, the direction of all right endeavour to secure respect for the workman as man. Not the least relevant aspect of his work upon architecture is his positively anthropomorphic view of every member and every stone as a live thing actually and continually doing work.

Meanwhile, without apprehension or intolerance, her studious husband observes Euphemia cutting a brilliant figure in the mingled Austrian and Italian society of the day. "She was allowed by everyone to be the *reine du bal*." It was an admirable *modus vivendi*. He could neglect her without fear that she would either be jealous of his work or disgrace his name. He himself was not faint in bearing, with an amused interest, an indulgent share of their social obligations, wherein he was, in turn, indulged. For at Marshal Radetsky's ball " there were musicians for the dancers, cards for the whist-players, sofas for the loungers, and a library for the readers, with all manner of valuable books laid open, so that instead of having to stand with my back to the wall in a hot room the whole time, I got a quiet seat – and a book of natural history."

During this time he was writing constantly to his father, explaining and protecting his growing self-confidence. " I don't think myself a great genius, but I believe I have genius ; something different from mere cleverness, for I am *not* clever in the sense that millions of people are – lawyers, physicians, and others. But there is the strong instinct in me, which I cannot analyse, to draw and describe the things I love – not for reputation, not for the good of others, not for my own advantage, but a sort of instinct like that for eating and drinking." This is his special *ingenium*, and it is well that he recognises that its validity comes from itself. He does not pretend that it arises from a desire to serve God ; but, having that desire, he can only fulfil it with this, his most real self. And it is entwined with another strand. His most intense interior life is connected with the threat of consumption. On the way home in 1845 he had the experience already recounted. Again, at Salisbury, his cough returned ; and now on Good Friday, 1852, he describes a similar recurrence. He began thinking over his past life, and how everything had been done for his own satisfaction, or to gratify his affections in pleasing his parents ; but nothing truly for the service of God. He resolved, therefore, to *act* as if the Bible *were* true. " And when I had done this I fell asleep directly. When I rose in the morning the

cold and cough were gone and though I was still
unwell, I felt a peace and spirit in me I had never
known before, at least to the same extent ; and
the next day I was quite well, and everything has
seemed to go right with me ever since. . . ."
Though it is evident to what prose-masters, and
how availingly, he has gone, these are the authen-
tic accents of the boy who " gave it up, on considering how many different things were wanted."
But he has learned his lesson. He has faced his
facts. " So I considered that I had now neither
pleasure in looking to my past life, nor any hope,
such as would be any comfort to me on a sick-bed,
of a future one. And I made up my mind that
this would never do." At this time he was giving
money liberally in charity ; while Effie was not
so entirely surrendered to gaiety as to neglect
visiting the poor and the sick.

But with this crisis there came both a more
discriminating tolerance in spirit, and the first
tentative move, emboldened by the reception of
his teachings, towards intervention in public
affairs. Of the first his appendix to the second
volume of *The Stones*, upon Idolatry, is sufficiently
indicative : " I have no manner of doubt that
half of the poor and untaught Christians who are
this day lying prostrate before crucifixes, Bam-
binos and Volto Santos, are finding more acceptance with God, than many Protestants who Idolize
nothing but their own opinions and their own
interest." And again : " But the unhappy

results among all religious sects, of the habit of allowing imaginative and poetical belief to take the place of deliberate, resolute and prosaic belief, have been fully and admirably traced by the author of the *Natural History of Enthusiasm*."

His invasion of public affairs actually led up to the letter of Good Friday, 1852, quoted above. The previous year had seen the publication of his pamphlet, *Notes on the Construction of Sheepfolds*, an appeal to Protestants to sink their differences ; to the growing High Church movement to renounce the substance of episcopacy, as they conceived it, and to the Presbyterians not to quarrel with its shadow. Neither the upper nor the nether millstone foresaw much flour from his incautious wheat. As a simple Bible Christian he held, quite consistently, that, if you honestly tried to do God's will, He would give you the light to do it by. But this beginning scarcely warranted the conclusion that you alone could be both right and entirely sincere. His avowal was that of the celebrated juror : " Eleven more obstinate men I have never met." Within a year he was to receive, as we have seen, the signal illumination, that nothing he had hitherto essayed had truly been in the service of God. During the winter he composed three letters to *The Times*, upon taxation, representation, and education, which he sent to his father to be forwarded, with his concurrence, to the editor. His father took exception to the tone of the letters and was made anxious by their matter. They were withheld and, by Good Friday, Ruskin achieved a humbler state of mind. But they were the germ of his future thought, nevertheless.

It was a further disappointment to him this summer (1852) that the National Gallery would not authorise him to purchase two fine Tintorettos, the *Marriage at Cana* and the *Crucifixion*, which he hoped to get, if the trustees would find £12,000. Thus far his influence was all on paper. His reputation stood high ; he was well received. But he had not that weight with any specialist opinion which could get any specific and tangible thing accomplished. To practising architects, artists and theologians, alike, he was an amateur, with an amateur's irresponsibility. He was itching to get his hand decisively upon the levers. And three events of 1851 were destined to provide some opportunity : his friendship with Maurice, initiated by *Notes on the Construction of Sheepfolds* ; the storm over the Pre-Raphaelites ; and the death of Turner.

# CHAPTER IV

EVEN before finishing *The Stones of Venice*, Ruskin was again giving special attention to painting. *Modern Painters* was still incomplete, and had done sole justice to Ideas which in his view were not the highest, Truth and Beauty. Turner's later manner, he found, had revealed a higher truth about light, its intrinsic brilliance, its glory. The Italian Primitives, again, and the Venetians, had displayed an exalted order of truth. And at this precise moment, when Impressionism was on its way, the Pre-Raphaelites launched their attack. It must be remembered that, in Ruskin's system, Turner was in actual advance of the Impressionists. These latter had a clearer understanding than Ruskin of the system of Ideas advanced by Locke and modified by Berkeley. They were painting the secondary and variable ideas conveyed to the eye by light, to the exclusion of ideas of the mind. And the variability of light gave them a wide field of effects to study. The same scene or building could, and even must, be quite differently rendered at different hours of the day. But Turner had portrayed the abiding moral excellence of light, as God's creature, in full blaze. In the first chapter of *The Stones of Venice*, after describing the Gothic figure of Hope in prayer, with the hand of God emerging from sunbeams above her, and the derivative Renaissance figure for which the sun remains, but the hand is gone, Ruskin asks : " Is not this a curious and striking type of the spirit which had then become dominant in the world, forgetting to see God's hand in the light He gave ? " This was exactly true of the Impressionists ; or rather, perhaps, they were grateful for the light, without caring for the excellence of what it illuminated.

The Pre-Raphaelites were not animated by Ruskin, but they were inspired by the same source at second hand, some engravings of frescoes in the Campo Santo at Pisa. The Brotherhood was founded in 1848, when the first two volumes of *Modern Painters* were published, but not *The Seven Lamps*. It was a youth-movement to which Hunt, Millais, and the Rossettis brought the whole force of their idealism – their sincerity, their romance, their poetry, their faith, their moral ardour. These were qualities which had been squeezed out of art by elderly technicians ; and they were dear to Ruskin. It was Dyce, in 1850, who forced Ruskin to appreciate *Christ in the House of His Parents*, and it was Millais, in the

following year, who sought Ruskin's championship, knowing his friendship for Patmore whose
sympathy the P.R.B. enjoyed. The critics were
savage and abusive and the professors so con-
demnatory that the revolutionaries were hissed in
the schools. By this time the first volume of *The
Stones* was out, and Ruskin's aid was powerful as
it was timely. He could both vindicate the
artists and find them patrons. The result of his
careful study of their work was the writing of two
letters to *The Times* during May, followed by his
pamphlet on Pre-Raphaelitism in the same year,
his Edinburgh lecture in 1853, and further letters
and numerous laudatory references throughout
his works. More momentous still was his intimacy
with the men themselves, especially with Millais,
whose personal charm engaged him deeply.

The Pre-Raphaelites were, and yet were not,
illustrators. They were dominated by literature,
not by the aspirations of painting to the Grand
Style. They took their subjects from the Bible,
from Shakespeare, Malory, Tennyson, Dante, and
so forth. But their pictures were less an aid than
an equivalent to literature. Rossetti's woodcuts
for *The Palace of Art* are sufficient evidence of that.
They bore witness to something akin to one of
Ruskin's truths of a higher order, the true life
opposed in *The Seven Lamps* to the life of custom
and caution and compromise. Further, it was
their expressed aim to bear witness to the actual
facts of objects depicted in their works. And

finally they revelled in colour. Ruskin felt it an
independent ratification of his theories, if such
were needed, that a kindred position had been
reached by a group of professional painters who
were prepared to maintain it at great personal
cost.

Ruskin returned from Venice in the summer of
1852, devoting the following winter to the second
and third volumes of *The Stones of Venice* and the
preparation of their plates. In 1853 he was to
deliver his first course of lectures, including one
on Pre-Raphaelitism, at Edinburgh. And he was
minded to keep a guiding hand on his protégés.
He went, therefore, to Glenfinlas for the summer,
accompanied by his wife and a friend of hers, and
also by both Millais, the ablest of the Pre-
Raphaelites, and his brother. The time was
spent in preparing the lectures. Eager theorising
about painting and architecture was illustrated
by vigorous practice. Acland, who had joined
them, instigated Millais' famous portrait of
Ruskin, neat as ever, pausing in his examination of the rocks of a mountain torrent. Another
outcome of this holiday was more momentous.
In the month when the lectures were published,
April 1854, Euphemia left her husband and
returned to her parents. In July, upon her suit,
which Ruskin did nothing to impede, the marriage
was annulled. In less than a year she was Millais'
wife. The worst aspect of Ruskin's altered circumstances was the exposure of so sensitive a

man to the shafts of malicious gossip. Although
his letters speak of her with affectionate pride,
his happiness was never deeply committed to
Euphemia's keeping, except in so far as she saved
him from courting misery elsewhere. On the
other hand, although the inevitable consequence
was a return to his parents, the gain in personal
freedom was unmistakable, both in the direct
enfranchisement of his mind and in the release
from social obligations. Furthermore, he was
offered an opportunity of behaving with the full
magnanimity of his nature ; and he took it. It
is one of life's most interesting disparities that
the man whose instinct is for selfish behaviour
can create sufficient occasions for its exercise,
while his opposite frequently cannot, without
officiousness, discover an adequate field for
generosity.

Though Ruskin's loss of hold on Millais was an
inevitable consequence, it was not immediate.
For Millais to become impatient of his champion's
conversion into a mentor was the natural process
of time ; and Ruskin could not evade the double
duty to his critical theory of both proclaiming his
supplanter's powers and voicing his disappointment at his misuse of them, even at the risk of
being thought, as Millais did think him, vindic-
tive. But his connexion with other Pre-
Raphaelites did not suffer. Hunt, it is true, was
embarrassed ; but Ruskin's friendship with Rossetti dates from the very month of Euphemia's

departure. Though cognisant of his work, despite its absence from the Academy, where the Brotherhood was principally assailed, Ruskin was unacquainted with the man. He wrote to Rossetti, protesting himself " yours respectfully " and asking permission to call. It was more than a year since W. M. Rossetti had last made an entry in the Pre-Raphaelite Journal. D. G. Rossetti had engaged himself to Elizabeth Siddal, and the ties which bound the original Brotherhood were loosened. Woolner was in Australia, Hunt in the East, Millais in the toils of the Academy.

Ruskin's approach to Rossetti was an altogether impulsive bid for a very complicated kind of solace. It was an invasion of a world very different from his own – romantic, necessitous, improvident, and touched with tragedy. The appeal of Rossetti's pictures to him was unambiguous ; an embassy from Dante and Giotto, bearing their authenticated portraits. In addition, the cause of art and the fact of Rossetti's genius rescued helpfulness from the imputation of officiousness ; it was in the ordinary course that a painter should welcome a patron. Elizabeth Siddal was Rossetti's pupil, as well as his model and his inspiration ; and Ruskin regarded her with affection, her work with enthusiasm, and the fact that she was a prey to his own enemy, consumption, with compassionate dismay. Their want of means, her illness, and Rossetti's anxiety were all delaying their marriage and impeding their work. What was more appropriate than that Ruskin should come to the rescue ? Up to a certain yearly figure he offered to purchase anything Rossetti sent him, if he liked it, at a proper price. Elizabeth should have an annual £150, and was not to overtax her strength, but should send him all her work. If its value exceeded her retainer, she should have the surplus ; if it fell short, no matter. Rossetti was forbidden to take great pains ; Ruskin wanted " the *easy* result of long and painful practice – a careless couple of sketches." Ida, as he elected to call her, was assured that " the plain *hard fact* is that I think you have genius." He wanted to save her life as he would a beautiful tree or a bit of a Gothic cathedral. The best service they could do the world was to accept his offer. He sent Elizabeth to Oxford, for Acland's medical attention, and was prepared to send her into the country to rest and recover her strength.

To Ruskin this relation was an invaluable outlet. These two were not of his world, and on the wings of such an offer he could represent himself in what light he chose. Extravagant rumours, amounting to real calumny, became current regarding his domestic crisis ; and in maintaining a resolute silence he became once again in his own mind the Marcolini of his adolescence, stern and aloof, more easily befriending than befriended, yet one whose heart was like a heaven. And his approach to Rossetti was characteristic :

" It is a very great, in the long-run the greatest,
misfortune of my life that on the whole my
relations, my cousins, and so forth, are persons
with whom I can have no sympathy, and that circumstances have always somehow or another kept
me out of the way of the people of whom I could
have made friends. So that I have no friendships
and no loves. . . . If you hear people say I am
utterly hard and cold, depend upon it it is
untrue."

He wooed them both, as of old, on paper. He
tasted the vicarious happiness of at once relieving
and sharing Rossetti's anxiety, of encouraging,
advising, and caring for a young girl, beautiful
and talented, whose love was another's, but whose
malady his own. But this time he expected to be
understood. To Rossetti's intelligence he could
explain himself without fear of ridicule ; his affection could be the more lavish for its disinterestedness ; the benefits he could offer were substantial ;
he stood to gain a position of benevolent authority.

After Elizabeth's tragic death the friendship
eventually lapsed. Rossetti grew morose and difficult, while the judicial tone of Ruskin's criticisms,
particularly in the case of Rossetti's poetry, was
less than tactful. Meanwhile, the critic had found
a new friend and protégé. His discourse is now
strangely at variance with his earlier mood :

" I am grateful for your love – but yet I do not
want love. I have had boundless love from many

Fr

people during my life. And in more than one
case that love has been my greatest calamity.
. . . I have boundlessly suffered from it. But the
thing, in any helpful degree, I have never been
able to get, except from two women of whom I
never see the only one I care for, and from
Edward Jones, is ' understanding.' "

Edward Jones was, of course, Burne-Jones, one of
the second Pre-Raphaelite group concerned in
decorating the Oxford Union and founding the
firm of Morris, Marshall, Faulkner & Co. As
undergraduates, Morris and Jones were both
deeply impressed by Ruskin's Edinburgh lectures
at the time of their delivery, and it was his lofty
view of art which enabled them to throw up their
High Church vocations with a quiet conscience.
Morris was far more fully Ruskin's disciple than
Jones. But he was robust, vigorous, romantic,
forthright, rowdy, and deliberately uncouth ;
and he was rich. He could take Ruskin's theories
and put them into practice, but the two were not
completely at ease. Jones, on the other hand,
was poor, delicate in health, docile, and tractable.
There was something fragile in his work which
recommended him to Ruskin. Morris was mys-
teriously native to the Middle Ages and retrieved
with uncanny certainty something of the life and
stuff of them – something discomforting. He
disconcerted Ruskin.

But that is an anticipation. In 1854 Rossetti

cemented the new friendship by joining Ruskin
and Lowes Dickinson in teaching at the Working
Men's College, initially in Red Lion Square,
later in Great Ormond Street. This college was
founded by F. D. Maurice and his friends for a
purpose which accorded so well with Ruskin's
teaching in the second volume of *The Stones of
Venice*, that they printed its famous sixth chapter
separately for distribution at the opening class.
Ruskin, who had received a prospectus, volun-
teered his services and taught elementary drawing and landscape. It was an attempt to make
the workman capable of being an artist in his
work and to give him some appreciation and share
of the culture from which he was being excluded.
And, again, it gave Ruskin, as did his work with
the students at the Architectural Museum, some
consciousness of using his influence in personal
contact as well as in the printed word. He denied,
in a letter to Rossetti, any motive of recovering
ground lost through rumours concerning his
private affairs. Such work was certainly more
congenial, and accorded better with his needs,
than the social activities of his married years. It
rescued him from the trivialities of his own class,
in whose serious work and responsibilities he had
no active share. Neither consciousness that his
writings satisfied himself, nor the figures of their
sales, could be as present and reassuring a proof
that he was having some effect, as could the
improvement in another man's work under his

immediate guidance. And he needed this re-
assurance.

Another tangible fruit of his labours was to
come in 1856 and the following years, as a result
of Turner's will. Turner died leaving his pictures
and sketches in some confusion and the pro-
visions of his will open to legal dispute, though his
intentions were tolerably plain. Ruskin was to
be an executor. Beyond the celebrated gesture of
leaving two pictures to hang beside two Claudes
in the National Gallery, Turner left to that Gallery all his finished pictures, to be housed in special
rooms named Turner's Gallery ; if this was not
accomplished within ten years, his own house
was to be used for this purpose. Meanwhile, the
whole contents of the house were to remain un-
disturbed. There were various small legacies,
and a bequest to the Royal Academy endowing
an annual dinner on his birthday and a Professorship of Landscape, with a Turner's Gold Medal
to be awarded in that branch from time to time.
The very considerable residue was bequeathed
to found a charitable institution for poor and
decayed male artists born in England, the lawful
issue of English parents.

Ruskin was hopeful of personally acquiring
many of the sketches and of designing and becoming curator of the gallery. But the will was con-
tested, and Turner's countrymen were " left to
bury, with threefold honour, his body in St.
Paul's, his pictures at Charing Cross, and his

purposes in Chancery." Ruskin refused to act,
and in 1856 a settlement was reached. The
National Gallery received the two named pictures,
and all other pictures, drawings and sketches in
whatever state. The residue, except £20,000 to
the Academy, went to console the next of kin.
Since the ninth year of George II it was unlawful
to arrest by quite these means the decay of poor
artists of lawful English birth.[1] But the sketches
were not to be dispersed, and Ruskin returned to
England to solicit from Palmerston the unsalaried
curatorship of a collection which embarrassed its
recipients. There were some 20,000 in all, and
Ruskin offered to sort and catalogue them and
mount 100 at his own cost, as an illustration of the
methods he advocated for their preservation.
Only after more than a year of arduous labour
was the sorting finally complete ; and it was a
grievous disappointment to Ruskin that most of
the sketches were left in bundles, just as he had
tied them, growing more mildewed with the
passage of time. But his mounting and housing
of such sketches as he could was work of visible
and lasting effect.

Ruskin's work as an art-teacher was not
limited to classes. He took infinite trouble in
giving lessons and advice by letter, and in the
winter of 1856 composed *The Elements of Drawing*,
in the form of three illustrated letters, followed

[1] The Charitable Uses Act, 9 Geo. II, c. 36. See Cook, *Life of Ruskin*, Vol. I, p. 415.

two years later by *The Elements of Perspective*. Meanwhile, from 1855 until 1859, he published his annual *Academy Notes* and in 1856 the third and fourth volumes of *Modern Painters*. Ten years, and ten such years, had passed since the second volume appeared. He no longer needed the support of his system of ideas, faculties, and formal arrangements. On his tour of 1854, after Euphemia left him, he received what he accounted the third of his direct calls from God ; the first such had been at Geneva in 1841, the second in the same place a year later. This, the third, was at Lucerne on July 2, 1854. In August he describes himself as " stronger in health, higher in hope, deeper in peace, than I have been for years." And it was true. Not only could he write with the increased confidence of heightened prestige and greatly reinforced knowledge, but he had lost a certain retiringness. It was too late to shrink from personal criticism, for his domestic crisis had subjected his private character to public scrutiny. Without boldness he was lost.

He began the third volume of *Modern Painters* by recapitulating his argument in the light of his added experience, reconciling, as in his pamphlet on Pre-Raphaelitism, his love of Turner with his hopes of the Pre-Raphaelites. And it must be noted that in Turner he was proclaiming a finished achievement, in the others rather the laying of a foundation, a new beginning. His

method is now historical. He points to pure
landscape as a new development in art and, after
explaining what he means by the Pathetic Fallacy
as the disaster of modern landscape, he gives a
history of classical, mediæval, and modern landscape, followed by his own theory of it. But
before doing so he must make his general position
clear by examining Reynolds' conception of the
Grand Style and opposing to it his own of the
Great Style ; this leads to a discussion of false
idealism underlying the first and true Idealism
appropriate to the second, with a final summing-
up of the Use of Pictures. In the greater part of
the argument, painting and poetry are treated as
a continuous whole and not as separate arts.
Granted sincerity, everything turns on the relation
of Truth and Beauty. To be *great*, art must have
a noble subject sincerely chosen ; that is to say,
the nobility of the artist's mind must be adequate
to his subject. After that, there must be as much
Beauty as is consistent with Truth, no more and
no less. It is the Pathetic Fallacy to falsify Truth
in the interests of Beauty or of feeling. While in
his first volume Ruskin appears to give Beauty a
higher rank than Truth, and while he nowhere
allows them to be identical, he nevertheless will
not countenance the slightest sacrifice of Truth
to Beauty. The apparent higher office of Beauty
is that it ennobles the mind already conversant
with Truth. Truth accompanied by Beauty is
therefore preferable to Truth alone. Behind

everything lies Ruskin's conviction that, whereas the exponents of the Grand Style professed to teach it, the Great Style cannot be taught in the schools. " It is the expression of the mind of a God-made great man."

His fourth volume is an exposition of the truth about mountains and their beauty, while the first two parts of the fifth volume deal similarly with leaves and clouds. This part of the work is supplementary to the discussion of the truths of nature which precedes any consideration of Beauty in Volume I.

A distinction must be made between Ruskin's teaching about art and his teaching of art. On his own showing, he could not teach greatness, but only point it out. *The Elements of Drawing* aims at discouraging tricks calculated to produce a grand effect and inculcates a method of study and practice based, he claims, on that of Leonardo, which will produce sound and accurate work. It endeavours by analysis to exhibit the beauty of nature and the merits of Turner's composition. More than that it cannot do. The *Academy Notes* must be regarded as part of his art-teaching, not as pure criticism. He dared not praise without at the same time warning his pupils against what he believed to be faults. Though he might help painters by purchase or by influencing patrons, he had put it out of his power to back them with unqualified praise. Before the *Notes* were discontinued he won a reputation,

difficult in his circumstances to avoid, for savagely
" sticking his tusk in."

Ruskin's especial insistence upon Truth and
his obliteration of any division between painting
and poetry are interesting in conjunction with
his own abandonment of poetry. The whole pre-
occupation with Truth and Beauty and Nobility
and the True Life had been more than an essay
in æsthetic philosophy. It brought him entirely
clear of his old false notions and set him tempor-
arily upon a firm foundation. For instance, he
could preach humility, because he had been more
than once profoundly humbled by the recogni-
tion of the truth, and he knew it to be the source
of his strength. But he made no false show of
humility. With all his gentleness in private, he
was dogmatic and savage enough in print. His
situation was reversed ; for, where he had once
lived powerfully in his own mind and used his
writing to manipulate experience and mould the
figure of himself in conformity with his ideas of
what was creditable, he now lived powerfully
in the world he had made his own, letting experience mould him and using his writing to shape his
ideas. And this was to break him in the end.
He had acquired altogether too dangerous an
honesty for one who did not yet know himself
fully.

Three other activities of this period call for
mention, each adding something to his practical
effect on the life about him : they were his

interest in the Oxford Museum, his lectures at
Manchester and elsewhere, and his introduction
to certain ladies.  The Oxford Museum had long
been demanded by Acland and other Oxford
scientists, to promote the study of natural science.
Both as Acland's friend and as one who had
greatly relied upon the importance of the laws of
nature, Ruskin favoured the project.  But the
building itself was to put his recent teaching into
practical effect.  In December of 1854 the work
was given to Benjamin Woodward – a friend of
Rossetti's – who had already, in building the new
library at Trinity College, Dublin, paid particular
attention to getting good designs for his decorative
details and allowed considerable initiative to his
stone-carvers.

While the main construction was somewhat
hampered by want of funds, so that even cast-
iron pillars had to be brought into use, the adorn-
ment of the building was in great part left to
private benefaction.  It was itself a history and a
text-book of natural science.  Its stone columns
were specimens of a wide range of geology, its
carvings represented varied species of the animal
and vegetable kingdoms, while its statues portrayed great scientists of the past.  Among its
mural decorations were the Mer de Glace and
the lava streams of Vesuvius.  It was an extension to secular uses of the Gothic custom of adorn-
ing religious buildings with religious sculpture.
But, by its implied relegation of religious subjects

to consecrated buildings, it was a betrayal. It made religion a department of life. The Middle Ages brought nature into their churches because it was created ; and Ruskin himself had insisted upon the rightness of Henry III in decorating his palace in Wiltshire with kings below and the Virgin and saints above, and in causing the story of Dives and Lazarus to preach from the windows of his great hall. Here, if anywhere, upon this salutary analogy, there should have been re-minders that the earth is the Lord's ; there should have been the Days of Creation and Noah's ark and Jonah and his whale ; and not too inconspicuous should have been the story of the woman who spent her all upon physicians and got no remedy. It was left to one of Woodward's imported Irish workmen, O'Shea, to test the humour and humility of the authorities and find them wanting. Fergusson, more solicitous for the dignity of his university than for the autonomy of art, began remonstrating with O'Shea for carving monkeys round a window at the bidding of the absent Woodward. The next day it was cats. Fergusson was alarmed and O'Shea was dismissed. But Acland found him, none the less, carving the front porch, for which the architect had given no design as yet. Asked what he was doing, the workman shouted above the noise of his own furious strokes : " Parrhots and owwls ! Parrhots and owwls ! Members of Convocation ! " Acland, alas, obliged him to deface them. At this same period, it may be remembered, Woodward built the Union Society's first debating-hall ; and when the Pre-Raphaelites came to decorate it, Morris' friends introduced into corners of his own ceiling design—now unfortunately lost—disrespectful portraits of the scarcely slender or well-groomed designer. But he was not a Member of Convocation.

Ruskin was assiduous in designing, suggesting, and encouraging, and even trying his hand at brick-laying. The total effect of so experimental a building as the Museum, designed to house a large number of departments and meet the requirements of their several professors, is less impressive than the testimony of the carvings to the value of Ruskin's theories, the direct appeal to nature, and the concession of initiative to the man who does the work.

Ruskin's lectures at this time, reprinted in *A Joy for Ever* and *The Two Paths*, were a direct challenge to the prevalent economic theory. From the very first he regarded the health of a nation's living art as a symptom of the health of national character throughout its whole society. He saw clearly enough that, to the economist, the abstract " hand " existed only in his labour, and that in that labour he was being robbed of the full exercise of his powers and responsibilities as a man. He discerned this tendency in the monotonous repetitions of Renaissance ornament coupled with the baseness of Renaissance

institutions ; and he began to demand, quite
logically, a state of society in which none should
be idle, none overworked, and every man's
inventiveness should contribute in its own degree
to the common art, and every man's leisure should
be ennobled by the enjoyment of that art. To
achieve this, it was quite evident that the spirit
of co-operation must replace that of competition ;
and co-operation must be guided by a central
authority. He began to press for wider general
education of the people, so that they might
appreciate art, as well as for the encouragement
of skill in its production, and for an increased
leisure for the people, involving some Government
interference with the operations of economic law.

The active years between 1854 and 1860 were
probably the best and most rewarding of Ruskin's
life. They saw the extension of his theory to its
full growth in its evident application to the whole
of national life. And with this extension came the
conclusion of his purely artistic thought, in the
last two parts of *Modern Painters*, which appeared
in 1860. This treatise on Ideas of Relation,
promised seventeen years before, falls into two
parts, dealing with Formal and Spiritual Invention. He represents the formal composition of a
picture as being like that of a live organic thing
in which every part, even to the least, has its
function and its purpose in the single unity. The
picture thus becomes, not only a balanced and
vital integration, but the very mirror of the unified

society in which each has his due place and exerts his full effort. But it is his treatment of spiritual invention which most fully reveals the conviction grounded in his personal experience. He demands unequivocally that art shall not be an Art of Escape, but shall face life, and the evil of it, frankly and exactly :

" However this may be in moral matters, with which I have nothing here to do, in my own field of enquiry the fact is so ; and all great and beautiful work has come of first gazing without shrinking into the darkness. . . . We must trace this fact through Greek, Venetian, and Dureresque art : we shall then see how the art of decline came of avoiding the evil and seeking pleasure only. . . ."

He demands, then, that art, if it is to be great, shall observe in its structure the principle of subordination on which the unity of the whole and its parts depends, and shall resolutely face the whole truth of life, both good and evil. Now, a man must do these two things in life : he must adjust himself to the scheme of things, and he must face his Good and Evil squarely without evasion. But need he do them in art ? Supposing him to do them intuitively and successfully in life, must he seek them consciously and with toil in art ? There is no compulsion. The suggestion is that, where they are done, art finds a greatness beside which the Grand Style is trivial. Ruskin is prepared to admit that, on other terms, you can have an art which is charming, interesting, or diverting, if that is all you want : for himself, he is interested in greatness in art and its relation to greatness of national character.

And these years, which finally determined the ground upon which he must take his stand, brought him other recognitions, of which the most seemingly trivial were to prove the most momentous. In 1858, to his great pride, he was among the first Honorary Students appointed by his college. His lectures had won the admiration of Miss Bell, of Winnington Hall, Cheshire, who induced him to become a visitor to the girls' school which she conducted there. Through his encouragement of amateur artists he made the acquaintance of Lady Waterford, who, in turn, introduced him to Mrs. La Touche, whose younger daughter, Rose, was then nine years old. Ruskin was thirty-nine.

# CHAPTER V

RUSKIN was now to challenge the most powerful interest of all, in a series of books upon which his popular fame chiefly rests. And he was to prove dangerous. He must be silenced or "his wild words will touch the springs of action in some hearts, and, ere we are aware, a moral floodgate may open and drown us all." Thus the *Manchester Examiner and Times* of October 2, 1860. The business world could hear without alarm an academic trial of strength between Ruskin and the economists, or his appeal to the Government to make the workers better equipped for their task. The immediate occasion of the *Manchester Examiner's* desire to put Ruskin "on the spot" was a series of articles in the *Cornhill*. He was not talking about art, but wages. Instead of saying, "If you want art you must allow the workman to be a complete human being," he was saying, "Unless you recognise that the 'hand' is a

human soul, you will have ' outbreaks of dis-
affection.' " He said it quite demurely, but the
demure can be dangerous. He mentioned " the
embarrassment caused by the late strikes of our
workmen." The hunt was up. The proprietors,
Ruskin's own publishers, obliged Thackeray to
stop the articles. Nevertheless, they brought out
the collected essays as *Unto This Last.* But the
*Cornhill* had its way to make. Ruskin's father,
though loyal, was disquieted, and many of his
friends were apprehensive. Carlyle, long his
captain and ally, was jubilant.

Undeterred, Ruskin prepared another series
of papers, which Froude, who believed there was
" something in it," undertook to risk in *Fraser's
Magazine.* These again were stopped, and
appeared later in the volume *Munera Pulveris.*
Ruskin, who was much abroad during the outcry,
began to contemplate living in exile and building
a house at Bonneville, on the top of a mountain.
He was in an agony at realising the existing state
of society and at finding himself not taken seriously, only abused and derided. The confirmation Bishop Colenso's writings afforded to his own
doubts of the literal truth of Scripture deepened
his disturbance of mind. He wanted to break
away from parents whose uncomprehending love
meant isolation in his own home ; but he could
not muster a sufficient callousness. One fact,
alone, appeared steadfast in a dissolving world :
a child of thirteen " put her fingers on the helm

G<small>R</small>

at the right time." It was Rose La Touche. He clutched at the innocence and promise of young girls, as at a rock amid the tides of avarice and dishonour sweeping the world. For them, as much as anybody, he wrote now, as in the days of *Friendship's Offering*, but with an altered heart. He began to ransack the classics, from which the Western pattern of nobility in great part derives.

His father's death in 1864 did much to lessen the strain. The elder man had never ceased to preside over his son's life and to embarrass him by a disappointed pride combined with a distrustful loyalty. Had he known it, Ruskin himself had no slight inclination to reduplicate this attitude. His letters to Rossetti avouch it. But his father's death obliterated all but the man's imperishable qualities, his generosity, his integrity, his singular charm. Nor was his mother, now eighty-three, left to his sole care. Joan Agnew, a distant cousin, coming upon a week's visit to Mrs. Ruskin, remained with her almost until her death seven years later.

All idea of settling abroad, or even, for a time, of journeys abroad, was abandoned, and the following years were increasingly active. He was approaching less dangerous ground. With his gloomy reflections somewhat mitigated by the radiant welcome of Winnington Hall, the more affirmative outlines of an ideal polity defined themselves in his thoughts. His admiration for the young tempted him away from the truth of the world's good and evil. Given such material, and a clean start, what new republic could not be planned ? It was possible to become less stiffly denunciatory, more admirably hortative. And in so doing he was lost. To exhort the young is quite harmless and even commendable ; it diverts attention from more dubious matters. For there is no clean start ; the young are gradually absorbed into the ranks of their seniors. Utopias infringe no ancient lights. Ruskin devoted himself to lecturing and to writing to the newspapers upon current events. His letters to the Press were entirely characteristic. His voice was raised on questions of foreign policy as well as of economics, and for the sake of a policy dictated by national honour, not by national interest. Of the lectures, *Sesame and Lilies*, delivered in 1864, appeared in 1865 ; *The Crown of Wild Olive* was published in 1866. To these must be added *The Cestus of Aglaia*, and *The Ethics of the Dust* and *Time and Tide by Weare and Tyne* : the first consisting of nine papers on the laws of art contributed to the *Art Journal*, the second of dialogues worked up from the mingled instruction and recreation of his visits to Winnington Hall, the third, written in 1867, of twenty-five letters to a working man (Thomas Dixon) of Sunderland on the laws of work. These latter, interestingly enough, were first published in the *Manchester Examiner*, his old enemy, and in the *Leeds Mercury*.

The first lecture in *Sesame and Lilies*, ostensibly

an exhortation upon good literature, soon becomes a trenchant and salutary denunciation of
a society that cares for nothing but money. The
second, a discussion of the education of women,
branches into an eloquent appeal to them for
some kind of compassion for the destitute, some
availing influence against the oppressor.    Together they form an attractive homily upon the
relations of the sexes.    But their idealism is
dangerously grounded upon their author's own
rather special requirements.    His attitude may be
symbolised by his insistence that a plant exists
for the sake of its flower, not of its fruit ; his dis-
regard of biological functions is complete.    By
this time, Ruskin was almost wholly " uncon-
verted," ever since his visit of 1858 to Turin, and
his disgust at the " little squeaking idiot," preach-
ing in the Waldensian chapel.    His conviction of
God's existence remained steadfast, but faith in
the guiding influence of pure and innocent
women was more present and more reassuring.
If only women would preserve that native rightness of heart, men could, and should, submit in
blind obedience to feminine instincts.    Nowhere
is Ruskin's fundamental weakness more engag-
ingly displayed.    The old Adam was in him ; he
was finally irresponsible.    He had been praised
and blamed, but never trusted.    He needed des-
perately to abdicate, to rely on some vaguer
guidance, as of parental authority, of biblical
authority, and now, most unfairly, of Young

Lady authority. He dared not be wrong, out and out. This was the more considerably to be regretted, as he had an emphatic tendency to be right.

Throughout the teaching of this period runs a strong doctrine of authority, based on his thoughts about money, about honour, and about work. At its simplest, he saw quite clearly that, while no one assesses the precise money value of being noble, we do set a price upon being useful ; and we drive as hard a bargain as we can. He believed usefulness to be intrinsically honourable, and he wanted it to be honoured. And the chief obstacle was the " law " of supply and demand. Ruskin beheld its blind operation producing a populace

" which has lost even the power and conception of reverence ; which exists only in the worship of itself – which can neither see anything beautiful around it, nor conceive anything virtuous above it; which has, towards all goodness and greatness, no other feelings than those of the lowest creatures – fear, hatred, or hunger ; a populace which has sunk below your appeal in their nature, as it has risen beyond your power in their multitude ; whom you can now no more charm than you can the adder, nor discipline, than you can the summer fly."

This is a fairly temperate statement of observable fact. " The people," he says, " have begun to

suspect that one particular form of this past mis-
government has been, that their masters have
set them to do all the work, and have themselves
taken all the wages . . . and as the luminous
public mind becomes gradually cognisant of these
facts, it will assuredly not suffer things to be
altogether arranged that way any more ; and the
devising of other ways will be an agitating business." If culture were not national from top to
bottom of society, it would become the symbol of
oppression, of an overt plunder or a sneaking
misappropriation ; the populace would not respect it, or even envy it ; they would destroy it,
or contemptuously sell it in the best market. Nor
is it advisable that the sobriety with which Ruskin
voices his expectations be allowed to obscure
their justice. The indications of his main rightness have grown no fainter since he discerned
them. To avert disaster, he requires a graded
and essentially feudal authority, which shall
recognise that taste is a moral question and shall
see to it that the nation is provided for materially
and spiritually, educated both in taste and learning, given work which is honourable, useful, and
beneficial to the worker, and veritably drilled
into good citizenship. And, to achieve this,
pecuniary reward is to be divorced from any
equivalency with services rendered, and distri-
buted on the same basis as in the parable : " I
will give unto this last even as unto thee." Usefulness is to be a point of honour, a part of that

strongly bonded and deeply inculcated connexion
between culture and nobility and work and
happiness.  The whole social structure is to be
as authoritarian as that of an army ; but it is to
be out of the reach of anyone in authority to be
seduced from duty by self-interest.  It is an attractive and reasonable polity, if only man were an
attractive and reasonable creature.

There is, however, something not to be toler-
ated in the very core of Ruskin's doctrine ; and
it springs directly from the central calamity of
Ruskin's life.  In 1866, near the time of her
eighteenth birthday and of his forty-seventh,
Ruskin proposed marriage to Rose La Touche.
And it is this which flaws the crystal of *Sesame and
Lilies*.  The book was not romantic thinking ;
it was special pleading.  For nine years the child
had been under his guidance, and he happy in
her affection.  In his " unconversion " he relied
with his whole weight upon innocence and goodness such as hers.  And in *Lilies* he wooed her on
paper to be his Egeria, the source and sanction of
his confidence.  The standards of ordinary life
lose all application here.  It is a picture by
Burne-Jones, Cophetua abdicating to the beggar-
maid, offering his own judgment to one whose
judgments he had himself formed, looking to
receive it again with increased validity as pro-
ceeding from one so innocent.  It would have
been a courageous marriage, but not altogether
preposterous, as between two such exceptional

persons. It might even have proved a success ;
Mrs. La Touche was so little disposed to influence
her child towards it that Rose could, and did,
take time for her decision. But it was never a
relation upon which to found an entire social
philosophy. The argument for the acceptance by
women of a point of view devised for them by
men is simply that they shall, from the first, hand
it on to their sons ; it is for the sake of continuity
and stability. But that they should accept it
simply in order to ratify it and hand it back to
their husbands is less surely tenable. And that
was what Ruskin, at heart, wanted. From the
ostensible fact of courtship, that the man, having
already made his choice, must leave all the decision to the instincts of his chosen one, he wanted
to advance to the position that in all things man,
having first educated woman to his purpose,
should surrender his judgment to her intuitions.
Even before biology made tatters of it, logic and
common sense were against it.

At least Ruskin was not dismissed. Rose
claimed three years in which to make sure of
herself. In the meantime, until she was twenty-
one, their friendship must endure the test of
separation. Next year she refused another
suitor and sent Ruskin a rose. He felt so sure of
her that his whole life was at peace. The waiting
would end in 1869, in which year he was
appointed Oxford's first Slade Professor of Fine
Art, becoming in 1871 an Honorary Fellow of

Corpus. The intervening years were spent in lecturing and public work, with a visit to Abbeville in 1868 and another to Switzerland and Italy in 1869, when he received the news of his appointment at Oxford. He was much occupied with minerals and botany and Greek mythology ; and to this time belong his Dublin lecture *The Mystery of Life and its Arts*, and *The Queen of the Air*, a study of the Greek myths of cloud and storm. *The Mystery of Life* was an appeal beyond his audience of two thousand people to the single person whose regard he most coveted. It did not simply seek, as aforetime, to impress by the brilliancy of his powers. Here, in her own country, he put forth the best of himself, in the desperate hope that Rose would appreciate a point of view she could not share. Rose was accomplished and precocious and, with all her charm, was given, even as a child, to solemn little fits when she walked " like a little white statue through the twilight woods " ; only her strength of Evangelical principles hindered her love. This unbelief of his alarmed her. If she could not reclaim him during probation, she had little hope of it after marriage. He entreats her to believe that, even without faith in a future life, his ideals need not fall short of hers ; that his time may be even more profitably spent in " rational, humble, and helpful action." He speaks of " the morbid corruption and waste of vital power in religious sentiment, by which the pure strength of that which should be the guiding soul of every nation, the splendour of its youthful manhood, and spotless light of its maidenhood, is averted or cast away."

" Let us do the work of men while we bear the form of them ; and, as we snatch our narrow portion of time out of Eternity, snatch also our narrow inheritance of passion out of immortality – even though our lives *be* as a vapour, that appeareth for a little time, and then vanisheth away."

This is, in the high Roman fashion, nobly spoken. But it was too greatly a reproof ; it availed him nothing. Later he was to write : " Last Friday about 12 o'clock at noon my mistress passed me and would not speak." For eight years he remained in alternate states of hope and fear, not from any coquetry of hers, but through her genuine perplexity which tortured her no less than him ; her malady deepened upon her. In 1874 there were " loveliest letters from Ireland " ; she returned to London and to his love. In May of the following year she died. Could he but have assured her that he loved God more than her, it might have saved her. But he could not commit himself to her conception of God. Neither could know how much the strain had told upon the other, how fixedly it impelled both to cling to what they held sure. And yet he could write, afterwards :

" I wanted my Rosie *here*. In heaven I mean to go and talk to Pythagoras and Socrates and Valerius Publicola. I shan't care a bit for Rosie there, she needn't think it. What will grey eyes and red cheeks be good for *there*? "

Ruskin's mind was too greatly shaken for professions of that kind to carry much weight. In the middle of his ordeal and soon after his Oxford appointment he suffered an additional and grievous shock in the loss of his mother, the all too dominant influence in his life. Rose stood to him for the assurance by all that was good in his own past that his present position was not denial but fulfilment of his past. Capitulation would have annulled the most illuminating passages of his life, and demolished the ascent to Pythagoras and Socrates and Valerius Publicola. There was a logic in it. Grey eyes and red cheeks in this life were good for the demonstration that real beauty and real goodness went hand in hand. But her constancy proved wellnigh as fatal to his mind as could any recusancy of his own.

The years opening with his professorship should have been the crown of Ruskin's achievement. In a sense, they were. They are packed with an amount of detail little serviceable to examine minutely here. He took deliberate refuge from the consciousness of his calamity in continuous hard work, as if to run off a deep-seated lameness like a superficial stiffness. The broad outline of his last thirty years must be kept in mind. His probation with Rose should have ended early in the year of his appointment. With a definite answer he could have gone forward at least knowing where he stood. He held his professorship from 1870–8, being twice re-elected during that period. He held it again from 1883–5, his friend Sir William Richmond resigning in his favour. In 1871 his mother died. Just previously he had bought Brantwood, his famous house at Coniston. In 1870 he founded the Company of St. George and began writing the famous series of letters, *Fors Clavigera*, which continued monthly until February 1878 and intermittingly until 1884. *Fors* was followed by the writing of *Præterita*, which occupied him from 1885 until 1889. The last eleven years of his life were spent quietly at Brantwood. But between 1870 and 1889 lies the period, unwatched by his parents, during which he owned Brantwood, delivered his Oxford lectures, was Master of the Company of St. George, and wrote *Fors* and *Præterita*. And it is slashed across by no less than seven serious attacks of brain-fever, the malady which had claimed Rose.

By the death of his parents, Ruskin became possessed of a very considerable sum of money, some £200,000 at least. A great deal was spent in benefactions to the study of art, to the Company of St. George, and to the relief of distress. It enabled his life to take the outward form by which he is most recently remembered. The condition of the poor was on Ruskin's conscience, on his mind, and, quite literally, on his brain. He used to preserve and cite in his writings contrasted press-cuttings of the miseries of the poor and the gaieties of the rich. Beyond question these tales of suffering and want, acting upon a nature acutely sensitive and compassionate, exaggerated the frequency and severity of his attacks. Desiring to pursue his work upon art with a quiet conscience, he could not simply regard it as his duty to Oxford to devote himself to his professorship. He must ransom himself. This he did by founding the Company of St. George and writing *Fors*. The Company was a real attempt to give his ideal practical effect. Firstly it was authoritarian. Under the Master were to be Marshals, each controlling a wide area ; under them, Landlords ; below these, again, agents, tenants, labourers, and tradespeople. It was to be financed by Companions, each of whom must ransom himself, as Ruskin did, by giving a tenth to the guild and living under the vow of St. George. Ruskin contributed £7,000, a tenth of his computed wealth. The capital was laid out principally in purchasing land and buildings. The tenants should pay a just rent, and this income be applied to the benefit of the land and its tenants, not to dividends for the Companions ; and Ruskin's own doctrine of wages was to operate. No machinery might replace handwork, or the motive power of wind and water, or animal-traction. Natural beauty and wild life were to be respected. The Companions avowed a trust in God and His law, and in the nobleness of human nature : they swore to labour honestly for their living and neither deceive nor hurt their fellows for gain or pleasure ; nor yet harm any living creature needlessly, or any beautiful thing ; they vowed to raise their bodies and souls daily to higher duty and happiness, not in competition, but in helpfulness ; and to obey faithfully all laws of their country and of St. George.

In the scheme's more Utopian elaboration, St. George was even to have his own coinage. But the scheme was by no means purely visionary. It was ill supported, but the money was there and was used. Land was purchased or presented, and worked upon the principles laid down. In connexion with the Company a museum was built at Sheffield, to implement the Master's educational ideas. The intention was not to form a solid colony in one neighbourhood, but to have lands and sanctuaries of wild life wherever sympathisers existed. The ideal would have been that great landowners should enrol themselves as Companions, take the vow, and administer their estates in accordance with it. It was more than a beginning ; it was an example. But it was not followed.

One aspect of the situation was that Ruskin, as first Master, assumed for himself and his successors an extremely autocratic control of the Company's funds, lands and liberties. He began, therefore, to address himself in *Fors* to the members and all whom he might win. He had to explain himself and the Company ; why he ought to be trusted and it ought to be supported. He had also to further the work of ransom by continuing to preach his doctrines and denounce the selfishness and wickedness of that human nature in whose real nobleness and majesty the Companions were pledged to believe. He secured freedom to write as he wished, without compromising his publishers, by arranging for George Allen – a joiner who had attended the Working Men's College and, becoming Ruskin's friend, had helped him to arrange and mount Turner's sketches – to print and distribute *Fors Clavigera* directly to the purchasers from Orpington in Kent. The experiment succeeded, and Allen took over Ruskin's previous publications from Messrs. Smith & Elder. *Fors* ranges over every conceivable topic. It contains fragments of autobiography, details of the constitutions of St. George, news of the Company's progress, writings about art, economics, religion, and history, denunciations of commercialism and of the clergy for wasting time and vital power in religious sentiment. Taken with *Præterita*, it constitutes "The Life and Opinions of John Ruskin," often penned with a savage trenchancy which delighted his master, Carlyle.

Ruskin continued writing to the Press on various subjects until 1878. These letters were collected and edited by Alexander Wedderburn and published under a title chosen by Ruskin, *Arrows of the Chase*. They are complementary to *Fors* and represent the author's point of view as mobilised for controversy ; everything he thought strongly or felt deeply on life as a whole lay behind his attitude on any one subject.

His tenure of the Slade Professorship involved teaching the elements of drawing as well as the principles of criticism. The Ruskin Drawing School owed its existence to his gift of £5,000 to endow a master. He further enriched it with a very extensive collection of prints and drawings, especially arranged with a view to instruction, He raided his own collection, and presented the university with drawings by the Italian masters, Turner, and the Pre-Raphaelites ; this in addition to his gift of Turners to both Oxford and Cambridge in 1861. Later he wrote *The Laws of Fesolé* for the school, to expound his system of drawing.

His first lectures began by relating art to the serious life in general, with a more technical discussion of line, light, and colour in painting. These, published as *Lectures on Art*, were followed by *Aratra Pentelici*, on Greek sculpture, illustrated by Greek coins. His much criticised public lecture on Michael Angelo and Tintoretto followed early in 1871. In that spring, Joan Agnew married Arthur Severn, the son of Joseph Severn, Keats' friend. Ruskin's old nurse, to whom he was devoted, died soon afterwards; he himself caught a severe chill at Matlock during the summer and came very near death; and in December his mother died. Her illness had prevented his return to Oxford in October. He now gave up the house at Denmark Hill, which had been the Ruskins' home since 1842, having acquired Brantwood and having a constant welcome at his old home at Herne Hill, where the Severns now lived. His lectures of 1872 dealt, in *The Eagle's Nest*, with the relation of art to science, and with Botticelli and the Florentine engravers in *Ariadne Florentina*, the result of a journey to Italy in that year. *Love's Meinie*, in the next year, discussed the plumage of birds, and *Val d'Arno*, in the autumn, Florentine art prior to 1253. In the following year, that of the famous road-making operations at Hinksey and the establishment of the tea-shop in Paddington, Ruskin visited Italy for the summer and lectured on mountain form and the schools of Florence on his return. It will be remembered that, this autumn, Rose La Touche returned to London and in the following May she died.

Enough has been said to indicate the range of subjects Ruskin was prepared, nominally, to discuss. But the range of his mind in these courses was infinitely wider. He poured into them the fruits of his researches into history, science,

HR

economics, and ethics, of his constant poring over Greek literature and of his continued study of painting itself. His tour of 1874 brought him to Assisi, for the careful study of Giotto on behalf of the Arundel Society, and restored his faith in the strength of the Primitives. Towards the end of *Modern Painters* he had begun to believe the early religious painters weaker than the great Venetians. But Assisi convinced him that their lacking a scientific theory of perspective and of light and shade underlay this misconception. So intimate was the connexion in his mind between art and faith, that with this discovery, under the influence of St. Francis, his religious feeling was rekindled. This change became more revolutionary when, after Rose's death, he visited Mrs. Cowper-Temple. He was, that winter, as so often in his moments of great illumination, in much anxiety for his health. In the spiritualistic atmosphere of his friend's house, Rose was descried standing beside her and again beside him. She assumed after her death a supernatural and sympathetic reality. He became friendly to the invocation of saints. In heaven she could accomplish all that was denied on earth. In this mood he reached Venice in 1876 to prepare a new edition of *The Stones* and study Carpaccio. The former task led to *St. Mark's Rest*, while the second resulted, in addition to his persuading the world to a juster estimate of Carpaccio's genius, in a mystical friendship with his St. Ursula. He spent much time copying the picture of her dream. "Last night," he wrote in *Fors*, "St. Ursula sent me her dianthus out of her bedroom window, with her love, by the hands of an Irish friend now staying here." This is no mere way of speaking ; it marks the intense significance with which life was being charged. It is not confusion, but a methodical fusion of three worlds, life, death, and art, into one realm, to the remedy of his bereavement. The ideal, as if by a transubstantiation, inhabited and transfigured mundane fact.

After valiant help in saving the remnants of St. Mark's from the ineffable Meduna, Ruskin resumed his work in England. His lectures that autumn were readings from *Modern Painters*, enthusiastically received. A visit to Prince Leopold at Windsor, early in the following year, and another to Gladstone at Hawarden, preceded his return to Brantwood, which he had left in November. He was living in great emotional stress, only lifting himself clear of the world of dreams by continuous hard work which must be revenged upon him in time. By February 17 he was "greatly pleased at some messages from Venice, and from other places . . . further away." Six days later he entered the delirium of his Long Dream, and for six weeks he continued so. He recovered and returned to work upon his book of botany, *Proserpina*. He returned also to face Whistler's action for libel.

In *Fors* of July 1877, Ruskin had noticed
Whistler's pictures at the Grosvenor Gallery in
terms almost identical with those against which
he defended Turner, salted with something of his
own personal idiom. " I never expected to hear
a coxcomb ask two hundred guineas for flinging
a pot of paint in the public's face." It was the
*Nocturne in Black and Gold.* Ruskin was unfit to
appear, and Burne-Jones gave evidence on his
behalf. After the trial, so often described,
Whistler was awarded a farthing damages without costs. Ruskin's own costs were £400, and
this result, the public fact of his having been
technically put in the wrong, at a cost of £400,
decided Ruskin to resign the professorship his
health no longer permitted him to sustain.
Ruskin's condemnation of Whistler was perfectly
consistent. Turner's lifelong fidelity to nature
had earned him a right not necessarily the pre-
rogative of younger men. Ruskin was schooled to
hold industry, not cleverness, deserving of reward.
But Whistler had affronted his critic by something
other than seemingly slap-dash methods. He had
brought down the curtain of night upon the visible
world in which St. Ursula dwelt with her dianthus.
He had darkened Ruskin's triple world.

Ruskin took no warning. He persisted in
exasperated controversy, no less than in work
that soothed. He drove himself, no harder than
employers held themselves entitled to drive their
workpeople, to the last vestige of his endurance.

The poorest return of strength seemed a call to fresh effort. In February 1881 and March 1882 delirium returned. He was relying upon the reality of the ministration of the good angels, the subject of an Oxford lecture reprinted in the *Nineteenth Century*, and was much heartened by the friendship of Cardinal Manning, himself tireless in the cause of social justice. He challenged a controversy with the Bishop of Manchester regarding usury, having begun to think all interest usurious. His lordship's reply and Ruskin's rejoinder appeared in the *Contemporary Review* of 1880. The bishop permitted himself the harshness of dismissing the rejoinder, though not publicly, as " the ravings of a lunatic." Ruskin was moving towards a sharper dislike of Protestantism, a broader tolerance of Rome, but he was no whit nearer submission to Rome. His unique sacrament was the ministration of the angels, in effect, the ministration of Rose and everything she represented. Nevertheless, the visible sign of this communion was Catholic art, a world which could be expounded for general application in the pages of *The Bible of Amiens*.

In 1880 he sanctioned his nomination for the Lord Rectorship of Glasgow University, in opposition to Bright. He could not identify himself whole-heartedly with the political issue, and his defeat was decisive. When actually elected Lord Rector of St. Andrews, nine years previously, he had been held disqualified by his Slade

Professorship. The winter of 1882 found him sufficiently recovered, in his own belief, to permit of his resuming that appointment ; re-elected in January, he held the chair until March 1885. His lectures comprised in *The Art of England* were too much dominated by his personal theories. He was not content to examine the aims of different schools and estimate their success. Everything was done to decry the artists of national decline ; and he was before his time, if not justified in his reasoning, in preferring Greek art of the period from Homer to Marathon to that of later periods. But less reassuring is his retreat from the contemplation of adult womanhood to the adulation of little-girlhood, which underlies this judgment, combined with his dismissal of Leighton and Alma-Tadema and his praise of Miss Alexander, Kate Greenaway, Tenniel, and so forth. The lectures on *The Pleasures of England* degenerated into a public show, and his friends did well to dissuade him from their continuance. Nothing but the extreme gravity of his disorder could excuse the production of St. Ursula as a type of Catholic witness and, in contrast, Bewick's pig and Mr. Stiggins as Protestant types, the earnest and the hypocritical. His resignation could not be, and was not, long delayed. It came in March 1885, upon the sanctioning of vivisection by the university. The more considered publication of these lectures reveals their value as an outline of the growth of Christian England.

Two other lectures demand especial notice, those on *The Storm Cloud of the Nineteenth Century*, delivered at the London Institution in February 1884. He took his perfectly just observation of industrial pollution of the air as a symbol of commercial pollution of the moral skies of England. None had observed the daylight sky more faithfully than he, or perceived this modern darkening with stricter accuracy. Probably none felt that other darkening with more intense foreboding, as it kept pace with the darkening of his own mind.

The danger was warded off by his happy work on the collection of minerals at South Kensington. But, in the July following his resignation, the storm broke. It was his fourth bout of brain-fever. The fifth followed a year later, the sixth in December 1888, the seventh in August 1889 ; and, though he lived until 1900, he was forced to lay his work aside for ever. The apparent wonder is that he surmounted so many crises ; but, despite their terrors, there was something remedial in these attacks themselves. They withdrew his conscious mind from its vexations. He was back in his childhood with his father and mother and his old nurse. He surrendered the attempt to break away, by the mediacy of Rose and St. Ursula and the ministration of angels, into the company of Pythagoras and Socrates and Valerius Publicola. But, like Elijah under the juniper-tree, he believed himself " alone in

conviction, in hope and in resolution, in the
wilderness of this modern world."

" Vacillating, foolish and miserably failing in
all my own conduct in life – and blown about
hopelessly by storms of passion – I, a man clothed
in soft raiment ; I, a reed shaken by the wind,
have yet this message to all men again intrusted
to me.    Behold, the axe is laid to the root of the
tree."

There had been defections from St. George, and
notable ones :   Cowper-Temple, Sir Thomas
Acland, Octavia Hill.   He found " no other man
in England, none in Europe," ready to take his
place.

But from an American, his old friend Charles
Eliot Norton, came the suggestion most friendly
to his peace : that he give his mind wholly to
the past and elaborate the autobiographical
fragments of *Fors*, with the aid of his diary, into a
book of memories.   The result was *Præterita*.   So
clearly did this counsel minister to the needs of
his inmost mind, that we cannot wonder at the
poise which accompanied its fulfilment.   *Præterita*,
for all its self-revelation, has a reticence extremely
agreeable in comparison with much less adult
autobiography ;   it is a quiet book.   The old
furies and fulminations are gone.   He is not
explaining himself to the world any longer.   He
begins to take his whole life in his hands, chapter
by chapter, and to consider the forces which made

him the man he was. He is, of necessity, most
confident of his analytical faculty, and, without
passion, in this late evening when the time for
resentment is over, he does his justice of praise
and blame to the parents whom, except in the
Long Dream, he cannot reach with visitation or
reward. It is his last fragile hold upon the balance
of the mind, this resolute detachment which any
too great recalcitrance against fortune must
infallibly destroy. If anyone were fortunate
enough to come to it first among all his writings,
it is, of all that has been written by him and about
him, the best and wisest introduction to the man.

And it is the best leave-taking, with the story of
Rose La Touche laid aside half told, to spend his
remaining powers in gratitude for the care with
which Mrs. Severn watched over these tormented
years and with which she was to surround the ten
years of quietude following upon his illness of
1889.

# CHAPTER VI

Victim of misguided view of life; enforced and impatient spectator – rhythm relative to the True Life – unity of morals, art, and economics pre-requisite to his self-assertion – necessarily antagonistic to gospel of survival of the fittest – excessive demands on art argue disappointed view of life – services to taste and the knowledge of art – lack of contact with contemporary thought – impatience of thought divorced from conduct; his eloquence – denial of active participation in the world leads to intense emotional participation – dissatisfaction with purely economic or political systems – his inconsistencies – his main rightness marred by his obsession – his real tragedy – his disinterestedness.

WE are a little shy to-day, and rightly so, of the enormous vogue which Ruskin once enjoyed among our elders. For, when we consider how violently he denounced our elders, it is natural to conclude that he has some legacy for us. If we can find it, we should do well to claim it. And if we should discover that we already enjoy a great part of it, a more friendly view of our benefactor might add the pleasures of gratitude to those of possession.

A brief recapitulation of the view of Ruskin taken in these pages might lead to something of the following shape. Firstly, he was the victim of a too conscientious and well-meaning application of principles which happened to be false. Secondly, he was in the most exemplary degree their victim, inasmuch as he was composed of

exceptional material, unhappily too ductile.  He
lent an amazing sensibility, industry, and com-
plaisance to the very forces which were preparing
his destruction.  And, thirdly, within the limitations of his thought, he understood his misfortune,
when it was too late, with painful clarity, and
stated it with admirable frankness.  Quite apart,
therefore, from his positive achievement, his life
is a document of unusual importance.  He was
the very type of the " good " boy who turns out
a failure, and he confused the issue by the magni-
tude of his apparent success.  This assuredly
demands investigation.  What did, in fact,
happen ?

Now, in the first place, Ruskin simply suc-
cumbed to a perverse doctrine of faculties coupled
with an unworkable theory of the difference
between man and the lower animals.  Assume
that, if faculties can most conveniently be discussed and classified as totally distinct from one
another, they can, therefore, be successfully
legislated for as unaffected by one another ;  add
to this the belief that the use of reason is a quite
separate faculty bestowed from above to differ-
entiate man from the unreflecting brutes, and you
reach the agreeable conclusion that man's highest
achievement is in the sphere of pure thought.
That this argument gains more colour from the
reasoning of successful men than from the success
of reasoning men is a distinction too little appre-
ciated.  Ruskin's mother, resolved that her son's

achievement should be the highest of this high
kind – thought employed in God's service – and
relying on his being carried forward by the
momentum of the Church, completely disorganised his participation in the life about him,
by stimulating his faculty for thought and stultify-
ing that of action. He could do nothing but
watch. And, the more he watched, the more he
was fascinated by the spectacle of men having
discretion to make even a small immediate and
tangible alteration in the world, such as sawyers
and paviours and men filling water-carts. His
whole life is a tormented endeavour to bond
himself into the ordinary give-and-take of the
world, and it establishes its own pronounced
rhythm, its rise and fall. In this rise and fall of
Ruskin's development, towards and away from
the " True Life," three double strands are twisted
together all the time. These are : firstly, the
connexion between his religious persuasion and
his view of art ; secondly, that between his
spiritual experience and his health ; thirdly, that
between his feelings and the truth or falsity of his
life. He begins with a simple acceptance of
Evangelical principles, a simple attachment of
his only direct feelings to art and observation, and
a complicated device for dealing with the feelings
he was not allowed to have, in an imaginary
world. The first change was to try to make his
feelings creditable and live up to them. The
second, after his health broke, was to have a

spiritual call to employ his time profitably, accompanied by the loss of his false world and an anxiety for the plight of human souls. As his spiritual experience is increased by a second call, he begins to find his doctrinal world false and to feel more anxiety about minds than souls ; art begins to be God's service. The fourth change, with the revelation at Pisa, unites art to his spiritual experience, and his doctrinal world vanishes. A fifth, with the discovery that his whole life is false, and of the importance of work, brings him to the top of his curve, his conception of the True Life. He now begins to have his effect on the world and to be anxious about material conditions, and to insist that the world's good and evil must be faced. At this point he is interested in strength in art, and his admiration shifts from the Primitives to the Venetians. The sixth change comes when he finds the evil intolerable and himself helpless and ridiculed. He has lost the support of his doctrinal position, and nothing avails ; unless innocence, in the person of Rose, can be induced to ratify his attitude. A seventh, when this fails, brings him back at Assisi to religious painting and spiritual experience. An eighth, on Rose's death, unites everything into a semi-mystical world, through which he hopes to reach the company of the wise and virtuous of antiquity. The ninth and last phase, after his illness of 1889, brings him back, through the company of his parents and nurse during his delirium, to a simple and quiet faith, such as governed his youth. This is an arbitrary simplification of a somewhat complex process, affected by the discharge of numerous duties amid a variety of personal relations.

But it indicates something of the reason why Ruskin could never allow morals and art and political economy to be entirely autonomous. At the top of his curve he identified his own true life with work, which forced him to demand the True Life for the workman also. And it was necessary for him to have the whole field in which to become his true self. A man is not truly himself unless he can make his own decisions and abide the consequences, without being cajoled, dissuaded, or circumvented. And that is moral action, choice with due regard of the consequences. It is also self-assertion. Ruskin's sole chance of self-assertion lay in his work, and in having that work respected and not distracted. One reason for respecting a man's work, that his livelihood depends on it, did not operate in his case, and he was obliged to raise his labour to the highest plane, the service of God and the cause of art. It was inevitable that he should become embroiled with economics and the conditions of labour, because the distinction between art and commercial work is that, while commerce requires work of the best standard compatible with its being ready when it is wanted and with its being performed by someone who can be dismissed and replaced as expediency dictates, art, on the other hand, must be the artist's absolute best of the unique kind of which he alone is capable, however long it takes and however bad a business proposition it may be. And only so can the artist assert himself as a moral agent in his work. And only if this teaching was both recognised as sincere and accepted as true could Ruskin begin to assert himself. And only under authority could there be a *beginning* of self-assertion, a transition from obedience to autonomy. Work, morality, sincerity, truth, authority, were absolutely essential to him before he could begin to be freely himself. Add to this the fact that Ruskin was entirely surrounded by goodness ; add, also, the impression to which lovers are prone and Greek philosophy lends countenance, that beauty and goodness go hand in hand ; remember, further, that the Socratic man covets the approbation of none but the good – and it becomes apparent that Ruskin must secure the unreserved approbation of the beautiful and the good before he can begin to be himself. St. Ursula must send him her dianthus, with her love. It is this personal necessity which gives its cohesion to the whole Ruskinian system. He was positive in assertion, because it was vital that he should secure belief ; and he was fundamentally unsure of himself, because, where he most needed it, he was not believed. It is the most fantastic mistake to regard Ruskin as an exponent of repressive respectability because he was a " moralist." His gospel meant freedom for a man to be his real self ; and he preached it because he himself never had it.

Now, the doctrine that this is a man's real need, and that he has an instinct for it which must be gratified, depends wholly on the belief that each man's need is compatible with his neighbour's. It was not possible for Ruskin to allow that any law of nature which affirms the struggle for existence as a fact could be lifted to the moral status of proposing its intensification as a duty. He was too deeply committed. It is perfectly clear that, being brought up to regard deficient animality and the absence of self-assertion as marks of goodness, he must inevitably have gone to the wall in any struggle for a living. His own analysis of his upbringing, pressed as far as he could safely press it, is of immense interest. And his demands in education are the fruit of bitter experience.

" A man entering into life should *accurately* know : what sort of a world he has got into ; what chances or reports there are of any other world besides this ; what kind of faculties he possesses ; what are the present state and wants of mankind ; what is his place in society ; and what are the readiest means in his power of attaining happiness and diffusing it. The man who knows these things, and who has had his will so subdued in the learning of them that he is ready to do what he knows he ought, I should call educated."

That is not wide of the mark.

When we turn to Ruskin's theory of art, we find it remarkably flexible in its development. One consequence of his position must be borne steadily in mind. Being unable to assume the importance of art, he was obliged to demand of great painters a general and not an esoteric kind of greatness. And, if his demands were excessive, he was right in his general principle, although, once again, he was led astray by the imagined importance of the conscious mind. Art, as he saw perfectly clearly, asserts its own freedom. It will not tolerate demands from outside. If he had been content to require that art should not bedevil life, he could be met with the quite sincere assurance that good art does nothing of the sort. But his positive requirement, that art shall be packed with ennobling ideas, actually contains the implication which he so forcefully deprecated. It does, in fact, imply that life itself is drained of its impulse to nobility, that

*The soldier's pole is fallen : young boys and girls*
*Are level now with men ; the odds is gone,*
*And there is nothing left remarkable*
*Beneath the visiting moon.*

If life is not ennobled by art, it will not be ennobled at all. That is practically where he stands.
    I<small>R</small>

He wants to find in art all the qualities which he
finds life too barren or too weak to proffer.   He
makes it, not merely serve, but actually *contain*
religion ;  and he obsesses it with a vast burden
of learning, as well as an ennobling mission.
The reaction, when it came, was not a question of
the nature of art, but of the freedom of art.   Because it was a service to the freedom of art, at
that time, to assert the right to shock the respect-
able, it began almost to seem intrinsically more
artistic to be pre-occupied with sin than with
virtue.   This curious disservice naturally won a
greater hold over a certain kind of public than
over any kind of artist.   But it favoured the misconception that, if sin were somehow alluring,
Ruskin was somehow wrong ;  as if he, or any
reasonable being, ever denied that sin was
alluring.   But it was the substantial achievement
of that age to make virtue duller than vice.   In
any event, if the burden of sin is heavy, it was a
good deal less bulky than virtue's upon the
shoulders of art.   It has a smaller corpus of
publishable erudition.   Ruskin seems to suppose
that the more you study and think about a thing
and become articulate about it, the more evidence
there is that you love it.   But this in itself is
simply the love of study and thought and utter-
ance.   A dumb dependence upon anything, an
unconscious fetching of strength from it, is
stronger proof.   The final test is not the ability to
chatter about a thing, but being utterly lost

without it. There is something in art from which,
to certain minds, there is a deep fetching of
strength ; and, mercifully, it is as almost completely beyond verbal capture as are the pro-
fundities of religious experience. It is communicable by its own means alone, and partakes
of the nature of ecstasy, in the most cautious
sense of that word.

But Ruskin's mere services to taste and the
knowledge of art, apart from his benefactions,
were inestimable. He is the personified contradic-
tion of Mr. Clive Bell's assurance that " people
who set out from the hypothesis that Sir Edwin
Landseer was the finest painter that ever lived
will feel no uneasiness about an æsthetic which
proves that Giotto was the worst." He actually
did set out from Landseer and arrive at Giotto,
because his whole personality was open to be
shaped by influences which are superficially a
matter of taste. And he arrived at, and rehabili-
tated, a handful of indubitably great masters who,
in his belief, enjoyed at that time the contempt
and neglect of the polite world. And he performed with credit the difficult task of shepherding
the nineteenth century through the necessity of
working out its immediate possibilities, as all
artistic possibilities must be worked out, to
exhaustion. But he was perfectly cognisant of,
and insisted on, the power of art to go back and
pick up other unexhausted possibilities. In the
long run, Whistler and his friends put Ruskin

out of court, as he foresaw, with their genius for publicity. Ruskin wrote in 1880 : " The only living art now left in England is Bill-sticking." Or, as a more recent writer phrases it, " publicity has replaced tradition." But in no attempt to replace art on a basis of principles can Ruskin be neglected with entire safety, if we remember how greatly his view of art was entangled with his personal problems, and how great has been the contribution to human thought since his day.

Ruskin worked in a considerable degree of isolation, partly because he distrusted his contemporaries and partly because his work had to consist of those personal discoveries which forwarded his own development. Most of his time not occupied in writing or teaching was given to studying the things he wanted to write about, rather than the works of other people who had written about them. If this direct contact gives him a freshness of point of view, it also causes him to duplicate much of the work that went on around him. He could arrive at conclusions germane to those of Comte or Kant, but in his own time and fashion. He was not a trained thinker and made no effort to keep pace with the trained thought of his time. He was oblivious and contemptuous of Hegel, for instance, and of Schopenhauer, and, except through Carlyle, was little subject to exterior influences.

His main recourse is to the thought of the past,

especially that which is haunted by the ideal of
nobility. Thinking is inextricably part of conduct. And as soon as philosophy begins to
realise that it is thinking about conduct, in the
hope of improving conduct, it discovers that its
first duty is to think about thought, in the hope,
not merely of improving it, but of making it a
basis of certainty. At this point it loses its hold
over conduct ; for conduct is improved by conduct, just as thought by thought. Ruskin was
very little patient of this state of affairs. An
ideal of conduct, not necessarily logical in all its
implications, but still one which can animate an
essentially illogical humanity, can be extracted
from the Bible without theology, or from Plato
without systematic thought. And, in the brevity
of our time and the urgency of our occasions, such
is often the best we can be accommodated with.
After all, his goal was the True Life, not true
thinking alone. And this accounts in some
measure for the eloquence which does him some
disservice to-day, as well as his inability to accept certain systems of political and economic
thought.

Ruskin is not unremitting in his eloquence,
nor always eloquent when his remarks are of most
interest or importance. But he has been sufficiently advertised for his eloquence to be con-
demned for it. It is true that he exhausted the
possibilities of eloquence, but on that account,
although he cannot always be read with pleasure,

he is not altogether to be blamed for using a method whose possibilities were not exhausted at the time. Indeed, when we come to read him at all fully, we find in him an unusual mastery of English. So far from being drugged with biblical cadences, he could model his style, time after time, upon masters of the seventeenth and eighteenth centuries. But such endeavours seemed to him an affectation. His powers of irony and vituperation are to be envied and enjoyed. He worked at enormous pressure. There was never time enough for what he wanted to do, to save this or that while it was still extant. And, often enough, he could only achieve fluency at the point where eloquence supervenes. What must not escape notice is the remarkable precision of almost every word. The trouble is that the feeling behind it is genuine. He says with some justice that no one before Rousseau could have felt, as that writer made it possible to feel, about landscape. But the real change is not in the feeling itself, but in making that feeling so formidably articulate, so menacingly communicable. Ruskin seldom used language purely to express ordered thought ; but to suggest that he could not do so is to mistake his power. He distrusted isolated thought. He could never quite do himself the service of one particular piece of hypocrisy, that of pretending to be the pure subject of knowledge. To do so involves one of two possible dichotomies, that a man should either split the true object of knowledge into two parts by separating himself from it, or else split himself in two and merely contemplate himself as part of that object. Ruskin did actually stand apart from the world, and it was precisely because he wanted to reunite himself with it that he became more and more the subject of feeling. He began life with very little depth of feeling ; but, the more he tried to identify himself with the world about him, the more acutely did he take to himself, with imaginative intensity, sufferings not properly his own. He represents the extreme limit to which the sympathetic awareness of the good and evil of the world can be pressed at the hazard of what he himself euphemistically termed " Nebuchadnezzar's bitter grass."

And for this same reason, his distrust of isolated thought, he could not embrace purely economic or political systems whole and alone. He kept it perfectly clear that neither materialism nor economic theory can, in itself and by itself, care about ultimate values. Neither, as a complete explanation of human history, can adduce out of itself the evidence of its own good faith. He demanded, therefore, that men should not simply be educated up to political or economic doctrine, but given a wide and general culture. Otherwise their opinion, as voters, was " not worth a rat's squeak."

Accordingly, it is not surprising to find him casting his net extraordinarily wide in search of truth. Many of his statements are mutually irreconcilable in isolation, and he boasted of his perfect readiness to contradict himself if, in so doing, he came nearer the truth. He must be judged, therefore, by the progress of his central thought, not by his *dicta*. And in his general position he is often the heir of the eighteenth century much more than the representative of the nineteenth. He refuted his antagonists, as Johnson refuted Berkeley, robustly, often with no very complete appreciation of what their contention really was. The comparison with Swift has become a commonplace. The mischief in him was Rousseau.

His estimate of the general trend of events has proved sufficiently prescient and acute. He set his face against almost every vested interest in the country, with no single axe of his own to grind, except that of discovering the True Life. He became exaggerated and absurd at the time of his becoming obsessed with Rose La Touche. His preposterous demands upon womanhood destroyed much of the positive aspect of his thought. But what he hated he commonly did well to hate, though his remedy was occasionally fantastic.

At this point we must distinguish between his real and his formal tragedy. Formally the tragedy is that of two spirits ; both, to the full of their apprehension, arduously good, both lovable and accomplished, each loving and needing the

other, yet kept apart by the very positiveness of
their qualities. But Ruskin's real personal
tragedy goes deeper. It was that he allowed
himself to feel the wrongs of others with an intensity vastly in excess of his power to remedy them.
The very urgency of his need for righting material
wrongs made him concentrate upon a religion of
humanitarianism and deprived him of a belief
which would have been very valuable to him :
that prayers and religious exercises are not mere
sentiment and anxiety after the individual soul,
but are the real *opus Dei* and do, by the intervention of grace, strengthen the active powers of
good in the world. Apart from the question of
whatever degree of objective truth animates this
belief, it would have quieted the unavailing fer-
ment of Ruskin's mind. But, great though the
sympathy between him and Manning was, he
could not embrace the teaching of a Church not
primarily devoted to the relief of material evils.
In the opposite direction, he could not join forces
with the one man capable of grasping Ruskin's
sword and wielding it with indomitable energy.
Ruskin forged Excalibur and plunged it into the
stone from which only Morris could have with-
drawn it whole. But Ruskin's native unsureness
shrank from the headstrong exuberance of the
more forceful man. He would not trust where
he could not manage. That was his tragedy,
that he took all the misery of the world into a
heart whose largeness was more evident than its

stoutness, and all the burden of righting it upon shoulders conspicuously frail.

The vested interests which Ruskin challenged were under no constraint to argue with him. He was a formidable antagonist; but, by over-throwing the balance of his mind in the intensity of his sympathy, he put it within their power to say that he was mad and therefore wrong. There is more case for claiming that he was right and therefore maddened. He was as disinterested as a man can be; his powers of observation were exceptionally wide and precise; his analysis, within the limitations of his assumptions, was of great sureness. And the problem over which he brooded is still tearing the world to pieces. How are the young to be trained? What is their true life? Are the parents to have a free hand, or is the Church to hold them responsible, or is the State to assume entire control? Everything returns to that. Ruskin himself was the victim of parental control at its best and at the same time its most disastrous, because entirely conscientious and radically mistaken; not that he was unduly driven along the intellectual road, but he was unduly hedged to it. The rest of him took its revenge upon his mind, because he had been trained to see clearly and feel keenly, and at the same time the whole machinery in him for doing anything to mend matters, except by seeing more clearly and explaining more fully, had been dis-connected and immobilised. But his view of the place of man in society is especially worth considering, because it is, of necessity, disinterested. He is compelled to desiderate a world with a minimum of pain, because all unmerited suffering raises its plangent echo in his own responsive being.

# BIBLIOGRAPHY

All Ruskin's works are published by Messrs. George Allen & Unwin in various formats, from the complete Library Edition, edited by E. T. Cook and Alexander Wedderburn, at £50, down to some single works at one shilling.

Acland, H. W., and Ruskin, J. : *The Oxford Museum*. 1893.

Burne-Jones, Lady : *Memorials of Edward Burne-Jones*. 2 vols. 1904.

Collingwood, W. G. : *Life and Work of John Ruskin*. 2 vols. 1893.

Cook, E. T. : *Life of Ruskin*. 2 vols. 1911.

Harrison, Frederic : *Ruskin*. 1902.

Hueffer, Ford Madox : *Ford Madox Brown, a Record of his Life and Works*. 1896.

Larg, David : *John Ruskin*. 1932.

MacDonald, Dr. Greville : *Reminiscences of a Specialist*. 1932.

Mallock, W. B. : *The New Republic ; or, Culture, Faith and Philosophy in an English Country House*. 1878.

Whistler, James A. MacNeill : *The Gentle Art of Making Enemies*. 1890.

Wilenski, R. H. : *John Ruskin*. 1933.

Williams-Ellis, Amabel : *The Tragedy of John Ruskin*. 1928.

Winwar, Frances : *The Rossettis and their Circle*. 1934. (Contains a very full bibliography.)